HOW TO INVEST
LIKE WARREN BUFFETT

To Peter,

Thanks for the support.

Here's to rational

investing the Warren

Buffett way.

Best
Alex Hogg

15/01/2016

# HOW TO
# INVEST
## LIKE
# WARREN
# BUFFETT

*Discover the Wisdom of the*
*World's Greatest Wealth Creator*

# ALEC HOGG

Jonathan Ball Publishers
Johannesburg & Cape Town

Published in South Africa in 2016 by
JONATHAN BALL PUBLISHERS
A division of Media24 Limited
PO Box 33977
Jeppestown
2043

ISBN 978-1-86842-715-4

Every effort has been made to trace the copyright holders and
to obtain their permission for the use of copyright material.
The publishers apologise for any errors or omissions and
would be grateful to be notified of any corrections that should
be incorporated in future editions of this book.

Twitter: www.twitter.com/JonathanBallPub
Facebook: www.facebook.com/JonathanBallPublishers
Blog: http://jonathanball.bookslive.co.za/

Cover by MR Design
Design and typesetting by Nazli Jacobs

Printed by **paarlmedia**, a division of Novus Holdings

Set in Warnock Pro

# Contents

# Appreciation

Warren Buffett was a great inspiration when I came back from my sabbatical in 2012.

Moneyweb, an internet publishing business that I started from a room above my garage in 1997 and listed on the stock market two years later, was supposed to have been my life's work. We were one of the few survivors of the dot.com crash. By 2010 the business was solid and its interests had expanded into radio and print, and into the global arena.

It had been a hard road, though, so I downscaled my activities by taking the decision to relocate to the KZN Midlands. My replacement as CEO saw Moneyweb as a vehicle through which to fulfil some lofty ambitions. He brought in a new controlling shareholder. The business changed into a very different animal.

After returning in 2012, it was soon obvious that my way of doing business clashed with this particular corporate – a printer and local newspaper publisher that liked the idea of owning Moneyweb's digital footprint. After triggering a lengthy notice period in my contract, I went on 'gardening leave' for eight months, and during that time did a lot of reading.

Included in the exercise was going over my notes from my many attendances at Berkshire Hathaway AGMs. It was inspiration all over again to read how Warren Buffett and Charlie Munger spontaneously answered questions from shareholders. The many quotations from Warren Buffett and Charlie Munger that you will encounter in this book are taken either from my own notes (covering eight AGMs and six press conferences) or from Berkshire Hathaway annual reports.

Without knowing it, Warren Buffett has been a mentor and teacher to me. It is a role he has played, mostly unwittingly, to many thousands around the world. He has enchanted us with his humility, honesty and wonderful example of how to live. Warren E Buffett deserves all the blessings he has received in his rich, full life – and all of those still to come.

ALEC HOGG
November 2015

# Introduction

A life of observation has taught me that the ancients were spot-on. Since humans first learnt how to document their thoughts on clay tablets, philosophers have believed members of our species fall into one of three categories. We are, they say, seekers of wisdom, wealth or fame. This book is aimed at the first group. Because it is about the lessons we can absorb from a man who personifies wisdom.

Wisdom can be acquired from many sources. Experience has always been the best teacher. We are hard-wired to learn from our own mistakes. But the truly blessed among us are those who possess humility. This is the key that unlocks our minds. Without this most underrated of assets, it is impossible for the lessons of others to be fully absorbed. So my recommendation is to open your mind as you embark on this journey.

My exposure to Warren E Buffett began in the northern hemisphere spring of 2005 when I joined 20 000 others on a pilgrimage to Omaha, Nebraska, in the heart of America's Midwest. For many of us, Omaha has become the modern version of Ancient Greece's Delphi. Except that it is the home of a real-life Oracle, and the place where, on the first Saturday in May, the investment world's grandfather hosts the annual general meeting (AGM) of his creation, the business conglomerate called Berkshire Hathaway.

For me, every one of my eight trips to Omaha has been an adventure – sometimes spiced with flight delays caused by extreme weather, or by the selection of inauspicious hotel accommodation. For years, my highlight was an invitation-only press conference on the Sunday afternoon. Sadly, that ended in 2011 after Buffett turned 80, but not before I'd harvested a treasure chest of autographed Berkshire memorabilia. Some of these form a collage mounted in my office, the focal point of which is the pic of a beaming yours truly flanked by Warren and his lifelong business partner, Charlie Munger.

The Berkshire AGM is unlike any other in the business world. Long before sunrise, queues stretch for kilometres around Omaha's convention centre. Devoted Buffett disciples don't just line up for the best seats.

The indoor arena's capacity is 18 500. Nowadays, with up to 40 000 pilgrims in attendance, those who arrive late for the event risk having to watch it from one of the video-linked rooms.

A press pass gets me away from the lines and into a skybox, with a clear view of the small stage. And getting there a little before breakfast lets me see the amazing sight of hundreds of besuited investors running for the best seats when the doors are unlocked at 7 am – the 'millionaire dash', as some wag termed it, because of the wealth Buffett's wisdom has created for thousands of his followers. By 7.30 every seat has been taken, some two hours before Warren and Charlie enter to a rockstar welcome.

The duo then spend the next five and a half hours chomping peanut brittle, swigging Coca-Cola from the can and answering questions, half selected from thousands of emails, the others from those lucky enough to have grabbed a spot at one of 13 microphones scattered around the arena. Occasionally an activist gets to grab a mic and, they hope, the spotlight. But they soon get the message from a restive crowd who've made the trip to learn, not to be preached to. Mercifully, most questions are well considered, triggering the host's sharing of his wisdom about investing, business and life.

So why do so many make the trip to this remote part of the USA?

Every industry has its thought leaders. Writers still worship William Shakespeare; filmmakers try to emulate Steven Spielberg; actors watch old Marlon Brando movies.

In the investment world, the man who stands head and shoulders above the pack is a modest American from the Midwest who is motivated by compounded returns – what he calls the Eighth Wonder of the World. Buffett steadfastly refuses to move away from his home town, where he lives in a modest house bought four decades back, laughs off any suggestion of trading in his unfashionable spectacles, and enjoys driving his old-model car along Omaha's wagon-wide roads.

Warren Buffett was born on 30 August 1930, so is a lot closer to his end than to his beginning. But he keeps getting better with age, making larger bets through Berkshire, now a $350-billion giant and the world's fifth most valuable listed company.

Berkshire Hathaway has become a model for entrepreneurs everywhere, including the world-beating Google, whose founders restructured their business to replicate Buffett's example.

Warren is worth around $70 billion and still owns a third of the business he has built from scratch since

1965. But when he dies, apart from a few billion for his family, the money will be injected into the Bill & Melinda Gates Foundation, because Buffett believes that wealth should be allocated where it will do the most good.

Apart from a share portfolio worth over $100 billion, there are 80-plus wholly owned Berkshire subsidiaries; ten would qualify for the Fortune 500 were they to be separately listed. A true conglomerate, Berkshire companies are involved in everything from insurance, railroads and producing energy to selling chocolates, houses and cowboy boots.

Like his successful conglomerate, Buffett thrives by challenging conventional thinking. He is ably abetted by fellow Omaha native, his long-time deputy chairman, confidant and sometime mentor, Charlie Munger.

On that first Saturday in May every year, the two wise owls answer questions from shareholders. The AGM's voting and official business rarely lasts more than a few minutes. But that's never been the purpose of the pilgrimage.

Almost by tradition, long-time AGM attendees craft questions that open the way for the two Midwestern grandfathers to share their homespun wisdom. It is when they start freewheeling that Buffett and Munger shine brightest, delighting their fans with old-fashioned logic and wisecracks.

This book brings together some of that genius. And shows another side to one of the world's wealthiest self-made billionaires. He is a man the likes of whom the world is unlikely to ever see again. Read on and enjoy.

# Hard-wired for Capitalism

Warren Edward Buffett was born, bred and still lives in Omaha, the biggest city in Nebraska and almost slap bang in the middle of the United States of America.

It is the 43rd largest city in the USA, with a population of just over 400 000, and has a major airport with connections to all the big cities in the country. As you walk into the airport, you're immediately made aware of Omaha's favourite son. There's a billboard quoting Warren Buffett that says: 'My advice: invest in yourself.' It's an advert for his alma mater, the University of Nebraska Omaha.

Although Nebraska is home to less than half a per cent of America's roughly 320 million people, Warren Buffett and Charlie Munger are by no means its only famous products. Actors Fred Astaire, Marlon Brando, Nick Nolte and James Coburn were all born in Omaha, as was civil rights activist Malcolm X.

But, for the most part, Omaha retains the charm, space and friendliness of a mid-sized US city. Apart from short spells in Washington, DC, and New York during his youth, Warren Buffett has never shown any desire to leave Omaha.

He learnt about money almost as soon as he could walk during regular visits to Buffett's, a family grocer, started in 1869 by his great-grandfather Sidney. In fact, had Warren not become an investor, and if his father hadn't been a stockbroker, he might have ended up in the family business – although Buffett says he'd have preferred to have been a journalist.

Warren was an early learner. As a six-year-old he would buy six-packs of Coca-Cola from Buffett's for 25 cents, go around the neighbourhood, and sell them for five cents each. When he was eight, Warren started reading his father Howard's investment books. He consumed those books voraciously and understood them well enough that, before his teens, his father allowed young Warren to chalk up prices on the Big Board at his stockbroking firm, Buffett, Sklenicka & Co.

Like many of us, Buffett started investing in shares before he really understood what he was buying. But as he was just 11 years old at the time, his excuse is better than most. The young Warren bought six shares in a business called Cities Services at a cost of $38 a share.

Within days the price had fallen to $27. Some time later it climbed back to $40 and, as many novices who've been through a bad experience tend to do, the lad sold out as soon as he was back in front. The price surged to over $200 almost immediately, teaching the youngster one of those valuable lessons he has accumulated through a lifetime of investing – patience.

The seven-year-older Charlie Munger would have applauded the youthful Buffett: 'You get an enormous advantage from starting early. Warren was a ferocious learner ... he got a lot early and his learning has continued. He is a much better investor today than ten years ago. In this field, you improve as you grow older.'

Another of Warren's early adventures was into horse racing, where he developed a talent for oddsmaking that would be refined to an art in later life. He and a friend produced a tip-sheet that they sold to punters at the local Ak-Sar-Ben racetrack until the officials stopped them. The young Buffett would also scoop up the piles of discarded losing tickets, often discovering some that had been thrown away in error.

Buffett idolised his father Howard, a Republican Congressman who was so principled that he once turned down an annual salary increase, voted by politicians for themselves, as he believed he hadn't earned it.

This respect ran so deep that Buffett refused to reveal

his own political allegiance to the opposition Democratic Party until after his father had died. Howard served four terms in Congress. After he was elected, in 1943, the family moved to Washington, DC.

While they were in Washington, Warren got newspaper delivery routes and soon started employing other kids to deliver the dailies while he acted as manager. He did so well with the paper routes that, at age 13, he started buying reconditioned pinball machines. The young Warren eventually owned seven pinball machines bought for $25 each. They were put into barber shops and generated $50 a week.

At one of the Berkshire AGMs, Buffett told us: 'I got half the capital I started with by delivering newspapers. I must have had 20 different businesses by the time I left high school. The best was a pinball machine business. The younger you are, the better. The age you were when you started your first business is correlated to success later on.'

He's living proof. In 1946, at the age of 16, Warren graduated from high school with savings of $6 000, the equivalent of $77 500 in today's money. Buffett is worth $70 billion today, the second-richest man on earth behind his close friend, Microsoft co-founder Bill Gates. He started early and just kept on learning.

# Benjamin Graham — and the Book
## that Changed Buffett's Life

Warren Buffett admits to having had many role models. The one who matters most for our purposes was born in 1894 as Benjamin Grossbaum, but is better known to the world as Benjamin Graham. In Buffett's own words: 'I knew Ben as my teacher, my employer and my friend. More than any other man except my father, he influenced my life.'

Graham's lasting legacy is his masterpiece, *The Intelligent Investor*, which Buffett describes as 'by far the best book on investing ever written.' It was first published in 1949, and Graham revised the book at fairly regular intervals, putting the fourth and final edition together three years before he died in 1976. You will find *The Intelligent Investor* listed in the Recommended Reading section at the end of this book.

His ideas have aged as well as one of Buffett's Omaha T-bone steaks. Two chapters in particular — Eight and

Twenty – are as relevant today as when Graham first started analysing individual shares shortly after the 1929 Wall Street Crash.

A stockbroker and university lecturer, Graham's name change was the result of the anti-Semitism then prevalent on Wall Street. It was only in the mid-1950s that Morgan Stanley (the investment bank founded by JP Morgan in 1935) employed its first Jew.

Benjamin Graham was the first man to provide a methodical way to analyse shares listed on this mysterious thing called the Stock Market. Up until that point, particularly in the run-up to the spectacular crash of 1929, shares were bought on tips or simple gut feel. Not much analysis went into the decisions to purchase or to sell.

Graham quantified the difference between investors and speculators in this way: investors bought shares only after thorough analysis revealed their capital would be safe and would generate a satisfactory return; speculators were those who bought in the hope of making a quick profit.

Back then, very few people understood that there was a difference between a share and the underlying company. In 1934, Benjamin Graham published a book called *Security Analysis*, co-written by David Dodd, which started the science of investing. It is now in its sixth edition. And in 1949 Graham published the book that Warren Buffett said changed his life. *The Intelligent Investor* created the backbone of Buffett's entire investment philosophy.

## Learning from 'the father of investing'

Benjamin Graham also taught a course at Columbia University. As a young man, Buffett enrolled at Columbia specifically to attend Graham's classes.

They called Graham 'the father of investing'. During 22 years of teaching, he gave an A+ to only one student. You can guess who that was.

Warren Buffett was 20 years old – younger than most of the other members in that class – and those who attended say it always ended up being a two-way conversation. Buffett talking to Graham. And vice versa.

Graham would say something. Buffett would put his hand up. 'Yes, sir. Yes. Yes. Me. Me,' and the two of them would have this lively conversation and the rest of the class would watch in awe.

## Buffett works for his idol

Getting back to the Buffett story, Warren says, 'If you go to a business school, forget about any lecturer who's teaching you formulas with Greek letters. The stories are more important. What's happened to a company – not just the success, but the failures as well.'

'That,' says Buffett, 'is how you learn.' That's why he reads so many annual reports.

He wanted to work for Benjamin Graham, but after he finished at Columbia University Benjamin Graham did not employ him. Warren even offered to work at the firm, Graham Newman, for free. But at that time it was one of the very few on Wall Street that employed Jews, so when it came to new staff the doors were only open for those of the Jewish faith. Graham wouldn't even take in his A+ student.

A couple of years later, things started loosening up. Graham phoned Buffett, who was in Omaha, and said, 'Come and work with me, young man', which he duly did. He worked with his hero for a couple of years.

But when Graham turned 61 he said, 'I'm out of here. I'm retiring,' and he duly did. Buffett, then aged 25, saw no reason to stay on Wall Street. He went back home to Omaha.

There are two major themes in *The Intelligent Investor*. The first, which remains paramount in everything Warren Buffett does – and should be in the way you think of investing – is called 'the margin of safety'. The second is the personification of price movements on stock markets, the fictional 'Mr Markets'.

## Cigar-butt investing

Benjamin Graham was also a highly conservative investor. He would buy companies or shares in companies only when they were ridiculously cheap.

Those who know about accounting will find this interesting. Graham completely ignored the value of the plant, the value of goodwill, and the value of equipment. He used the current assets figure and subtracted current liabilities to end with net current assets. And then he would pay only two-thirds of the value of the net current assets.

In everyday language, that means he would only buy shares that were dirt-cheap. What he often called 'cigar butts'.

In those days, rich people were often portrayed as smoking cigars – think of the old cartoons or the famous Rich Uncle Pennybags in the board game Monopoly. They would never quite finish their cigars. If you're rich enough, you leave the last puff for the poor guy who can't afford a smoke. Throw it on the ground, and someone will pick it up and have that one puff. That was the cigar butt.

Graham applied the cigar-butt principle to businesses and shares. He bought shares only when they were down and out. They got to a low level, but they would have one last little uptick. Cigar-butt investing also worked really well for Buffett, specifically when he was managing a small portfolio.

Buffett writes in the 2014 Berkshire annual report: 'The many dozens of free puffs I obtained (on cigar butts) in the 1950s made that decade by far the best in my life for both relative and absolute investment performance. But a major weakness in this approach gradually became apparent: Cigar-butt investing was scalable only to a point. With large sums, it would never work well.'

Even when Buffett's returns were his best ever, he made a few exceptions to cigar butts, auto insurer GEICO being the most obvious example. And as his investment approach matured, he appreciated that buying poor businesses at cheap prices was not a sustainable process. As Buffett explains: 'Selecting a marriage partner clearly requires more demanding criteria than does dating.'

It took Charlie Munger's intervention to break Buffett's cigar-butt addiction. As Warren reflects: 'Altering my behaviour is not an easy task (ask my family). I had enjoyed reasonable success without Charlie's input, so why would I listen to a lawyer who had never spent a day in business school (when, ahem, I had attended *three*)?

'But Charlie never tired of repeating his maxims about

business and investing to me, and his logic was irrefutable. Consequently, Berkshire was built to Charlie's blueprint. The blueprint was simple: Forget what you know about buying fair businesses at wonderful prices, instead, buy wonderful businesses at fair prices.'

# The Margin of Safety

Mark Twain's travel book *Following the Equator*, published in 1897, is mostly a reflection of his anger at the exploitation by European powers of far-flung parts of the world. But it also contains some excellent advice for investors.

October, Twain suggested, is 'one of the peculiarly dangerous months to speculate in stocks. The others are July, January, September, April, November, May, March, June, December, August and February.' In the same treatise, Twain writes: 'There are two times in a man's life when he should not speculate: when he can't afford it and when he can.'

This financial conservatism was learnt the hard way. In that book, the last of his best-sellers, the legendary author born Samuel L Clemens would have been reflecting on his own experiences of squandering his fortune. He had earlier made a succession of bad investments in new inventions, capping it all by running his own publishing company into the ground. Mark Twain eventually went bankrupt, and had to start again late in life by travelling around the world on lecture tours.

It was during this stage of his life that Twain apparently invented the term 'margin of safety' when advising others on how to learn from his mistakes. Twain's last home, Stormfield, where he died in 1910, is on a hill surrounded by forest near Redding, Connecticut, and reflects the conservatism of his later life. It's a comfortable yet modest abode, easily affordable for the financially rehabilitated writer who left an estate worth around $12 million in today's money.

So what is this 'margin of safety' that Twain apparently invented, that Benjamin Graham amplified, and that Warren Buffett popularised? That master of succinctness, Charlie Munger, says it boils down to getting more value than you're paying for. I like that.

When we invest in stocks or bonds, each of us can develop an ability to look at balance sheets, income statements and cash-flow statements, to read the annual reports and then to make up our own minds on what a company is worth. Not what the shares or the bonds themselves are worth, but the value of the underlying company.

This is what we term 'intrinsic value'. You don't need to have an exact number; in fact, it's best to use a range for the intrinsic value. The really important part comes once you have a worked out the intrinsic value number. And once you have the number never, but never, buy into a company when its shares are trading at or above that intrinsic value.

Why? Because then there's no margin of safety. No cushion to ride out the volatility that is an integral part of stock markets.

The margin of safety, Warren Buffett believes, is 'the central concept of investment'. As Benjamin Graham wrote: 'The Margin of Safety is always dependent on the price paid. It will be large at one price; smaller at a higher price; and non-existent at a higher price than that.' And the higher this margin of safety, the less the risk of falling foul of Rule Number 1: Don't Lose Money.

Think of it this way. Take something whose value you know pretty well, say a house you've visited often – like your next-door neighbour's home. Let's presume it's similar to yours, which is worth $2 million. If your neighbour decides to move and offers the house to you as an investment at, say, $2 million, it's unlikely to excite you. But if he needs cash in a hurry and says you can have it for $1 million, the sensible thing would be to tie him down and force him to sign now.

At a price of $1 million for a property that you know

is worth $2 million, you're buying in with a chunky margin of safety. Even if house prices drop or the market slows and you're forced to hold onto the house for a while, that 50 per cent price cushion will ensure you eventually sell out at a profit.

As a highly conservative investor, Benjamin Graham liked a massive margin of safety. He'd never dream of buying into a business at anything more than two-thirds of its intrinsic value – and he preferred it to be much bigger. Those were the days!

The kind of opportunities Graham sought still emerge after market crashes, but, because of wider and easier distribution of information nowadays, are rare in normal conditions. Nowadays a margin of safety above 20 per cent usually suffices. Not the one-third or higher that Graham insisted upon.

Actually calculating intrinsic value, however, is open to interpretation. It can be based on the most detailed discounted cash-flow analysis, which only highly trained investment analysts are qualified to determine, to using net asset values stated in the company's balance sheet.

Buffett describes intrinsic value as counting back the future amount of cash that can be generated by the business between now and Judgment Day. This is not to be confused with dividends. He is referring to the free cash the business gets to keep after paying all its expenses and allocating what's needed to be reinvested to keep the business running.

Thankfully, financial directors of most public companies understand the concept and help us by providing a figure described as 'free cash flow'. This is the amount of cash produced annually by the business that directors and management are 'free' to allocate – through acquiring other companies, buying back shares or paying dividends.

Provided managers do this well, the 'free cash flow' that is generated every year will keep adding to the value received by investors. Quite how much value depends on how well the management allocates this precious resource. Which is why professionals invest so much time assessing the competence (or otherwise) of company executives.

Once you have the free cash-flow figure, plug it into an Excel spreadsheet and make a reasonable estimate of future growth rates, it becomes relatively easy to work out a range for the intrinsic value of a company. But please remember it's only a rough guide. Spreadsheet investing is one of the most dangerous pursuits known to humanity. So use the number as a tool, not an absolute measure.

To this point, when Judgment Day arrives is anyone's guess, but you get the idea of what Buffett wants us to grasp: it is the cash a business generates in its lifetime that determines its value. Nothing more. Not fancy projections about the economy, the sector or the supposed brilliance of management. Buffett is telling us to ignore the hype. Too many companies with great potential end up in the knacker's yard.

Investment analysts often work for organisations that are in the business of selling shares in companies. That tends to make them rather flexible when deciding how many years to use when calculating Judgment Day. During stock market booms, the period is often pushed out to justify Mr Market's excessive valuations. Buffett, however, sticks to ten years no matter what the market conditions. Which is why the Oracle of Omaha always seems to have a great feel for valuations at times when the rest of the financial world is going crazy.

Here's a quick example that you can apply to work out your own intrinsic value on any publicly listed stock.

Let's assume this year's free cash flow from your target company is $100 million. You are considering investing in the business because it is well managed and has delivered a steady growth rate of ten per cent a year, and you think it has a great chance of continuing to do so in future.

An Excel spreadsheet will quickly show you that if your ten per cent growth estimate is correct, this business will deliver $1 594 million in free cash flow over the next decade. The value of the company in ten years' time will be a multiple of that $1 594. Based on the market's long-term averages, you're safe setting a multiple of 12. So a simple calculation brings you to an intrinsic value for the company you're considering of $19 128 million (i.e. $1 594 x 12).

But before buying the share, there is one more very important person to meet – Mr Share Market's brother, Mr Bond Market. He's also afflicted with manic depression, but not quite as badly as his erratic brother. And instead of shares, his attention is focused on debt instruments. The difference is as simple as it sounds: equity is ownership of the company itself; bonds are the business's tradable borrowings.

All investment opportunities are interrelated because each of them competes for our money. Their appeal is compared through risk and return. The higher the chance of losing part or all of our money, the greater the yield needs to be. So before buying a share, even one as attractive as the one we uncovered above, we need to be sure it is better than other options in other markets.

In simplistic terms, cash is the safest bet. A $100 note can always be exchanged for $100 worth of goods. But for as long as you hold it in your hand, it won't grow to be worth anything more than $100. Invest that Benjamin Franklin in a reputable bank and at the end of a year you'll get back your $100 plus a few dollars in interest. Exactly how many dollars depends on the general level of interest rates and the risk of the bank going bust – the lower that risk, the less the bank has to offer to attract deposits.

The global bond market works in the same way, with prices of bonds adjusting to reflect the risks investors perceive they're taking. The benchmark for any country is the rate payable on government bonds – the market's assessment of that nation's financial position and the risks unique to it, such as political stability, and its future inflation and interest rates.

As state debt is the ultimate risk in any country, the yield available on all other bonds will trade at a premium to that rate. And, logically, so does the forecast return on every other asset in that financial system. Especially shares in companies, which carry a higher risk than the government bond rate – because before you lose money on a state going bust, most of that nation's companies will have gone that way first.

During this discussion we've also introduced the significance of interest rates to share prices. It's worth dwelling on this briefly.

Interest rate trends have for generations provided the most accurate indicator for share prices. When interest rates fall, share prices rise. It's all rather logical. The more attractive the risk-free yield that's offered via interest rates, the less the incentive to buy shares.

Why invest in a share yielding five per cent on earnings when you can get, say, eight per cent risk-free from the bank? But when the interest rate falls to three per cent, shares become attractive. Which is one of the obvious reasons why share prices have done so well during the era of quantitative easing (QE), when money was pumped into the system by central banks, dropping interest rates in developed economies close to zero. And why equity markets get scared stiff at the mention of interest rates rising.

Make this one of your credos: buy and stay invested in shares when interest rates are in a declining trend or low and staying there. No matter how exciting the return you have made, while these conditions exist don't be tempted to take profits too quickly. But start building up cash or even head for the exit (even consider cashing in) when interest rates start rising. Few catch the absolute top or bottom of the interest rate cycle. But tailoring your share market exposure to fall into line with it is certain to enhance returns over the longer term.

Buffett believes that, provided they avoid acting on impulse, private investors have a distinct advantage over professionals: 'You can make very high returns with small sums of money because there are just so many more opportunities when you aren't running a big portfolio. If Charlie and I were in a position where we'd be investing $20 000, $100 000 or even $1 million, we would find things that would give us very high returns with little chance of going down. There won't be any scarcity of opportunities.'

The Oracle of Omaha also talks about the importance of staying curious, but warns that 'the biggest thing is to have something in your programme where you don't lose a lot. Avoiding catastrophes is the most important part of investing.'

Rule Number 1 in investing, says Buffett, is don't lose money. Rule Number 2 is to never forget Rule Number 1. A healthy margin of safety on every investment you consider is the best possible way to keep you in the groove of making money from your share portfolio.

# Mr Market – Don't Serve Him

My favourite edition of Benjamin Graham's classic investment book is the one that includes commentary by Jason Zweig, a financial journalist who has been writing about investing for major US publications since the late 1980s. Zweig opens his commentary on Chapter Eight with a wonderful quote from the Roman emperor/ philosopher Marcus Aurelius. It's the perfect introduction to one of two key chapters in *The Intelligent Investor*.

In *Meditations*, Marcus Aurelius wrote: 'The happiness of those who want to be popular depends on others; the happiness of those who seek pleasure fluctuates with moods outside their control; but the happiness of the wise grows out of their own free acts.'

Chapter Eight focuses on one of the two key messages in Graham's masterpiece. Titled 'The Investor and Market Fluctuations', it introduces us to 'Mr Market', a fictional character who is the best illustration I've come across to understand share price fluctuations and how to take advantage of them.

Logic tells us, Graham explains, that there are two ways to take advantage of fluctuations in share markets – either through timing or pricing. The first, he continues, is impossible to get right consistently as there is simply too much competition and too many variables. Trying to time your entry and exit from stock markets, he concludes, is too difficult.

But pricing, on the other hand, presents an opportunity for the intelligent investor. It requires homework and an assessment of what a particular company is worth. And then to understand that the dancing of Mr Market will affect the popularity of individual stocks and, as a consequence, make them either expensive or cheap relative to what they're really worth. To take advantage of pricing, in other words, is to calculate the intrinsic value of a company, and then to wait as its popularity among investors either wanes or soars – and to take advantage of these mood swings to buy or sell.

Graham wrote: 'By pricing we mean the endeavour to buy stocks when they are quoted below their fair value and to sell them when they rise above such value. A less ambitious form of pricing is the simple effort to make sure that when you buy you do not pay too much for your stocks.'

Ever the believer in simplicity and first avoiding mistakes, Warren Buffett's investment process falls squarely into the second category. As his recommended period for owning a stock is at least five years and preferably forever, after deciding he likes the business Buffett will exercise patience, ensuring that the share price falls before placing his 'buy' order. Mr Market guarantees that Buffett – and the rest of us – always get the opportunity to buy a slice of any company identified as a great investment.

*'We want businesses with visibility especially five years down the line.'*

So who is Mr Market? The best way of understanding him is to use an example. Imagine you own half of a small business, a private company worth, say, $100 000. Your partner in the business is a manic-depressive who refuses medication. And he loves trading. And every day he offers you a price at which he'll buy your stake, or sell you his.

Some days, Graham wrote, Mr Market's valuation seems plausible. But at other times he becomes enthusiastic or fearful and proposes silly values. As the sane one in the relationship, the rational approach is selling to Mr Market when he's in a manic phase and bids for your half at a ridiculously high price (say, $200 000). And buying him out when he hits depression and quotes a very low price (say, $20 000).

For the rest of the time, Graham observed, you'd be wiser forming your own opinion of the value based on factual reports from the company about its operational and financial position. The intelligent investor should never forget this principle: you can take advantage of the daily price quoted on the stock exchange – your own Mr Market – or ignore it.

Buffett is old school. He keeps up with the news, reading half a dozen newspapers a day. That way he keeps abreast of broad market moves, and dramatic ones in certain stocks. These are important because they inform us about structural changes that might be happening within businesses. Price movements shouldn't be ignored, but there is usually plenty of warning when a company goes into a decline, and Graham's advice to only 'give it a good hard look from time to time' will suffice.

Although he owns a computer, Buffett doesn't have a terminal flashing price movements. He restricts its usage to playing online bridge, having learnt from his own teacher to stay far away from the daily machinations of share prices. That way, he avoids getting caught up in Mr Market's hysteria.

Back to the example of your small business partnership with Mr Market. The major advantage for an owner of a listed share is the option it provides. You can follow the Buffett maxim of acting like a part-owner of the business for life – or treat the shares as being for sale at any time at a price you like.

The true investor is very rarely *forced* to sell his shares – exceptions being in takeovers when 90 per cent of other shareholders vote to sell at a price being bid from outside that they believe is acceptable. For the rest of the time, investors are able to disregard completely the quoted market price and, said Graham, 'pay attention and act on it only so far as it suits your book – no more'.

Graham warned: 'The investor who permits himself to be unduly worried by unjustified market changes is transforming his basic advantage into a disadvantage'. In other words, by letting Mr Market influence decisions, you are allowing yourself to be affected by what Buffett describes as 'other peoples' errors of judgment'.

Daily share price quotes are for convenience only. Approaching the share market in this way – recognising Mr Market for what he is – means you'll never buy a stock *because* it has risen, or sell one *because* it has fallen.

Graham reckoned the most obvious distinction between an investor and a speculator was their attitude towards stock market movements. An investor's goal must be to buy shares when they are available at a suitable price and to hold them for the dividend flow. Price movements are simply an indication of when it is best to buy or not to buy. Speculators want to discover a way to buy at a price below where they can later sell the stock, so they follow the momentum and believe in things like 'the trend is your friend'.

The author of *The Intelligent Investor* added: 'The investor with a portfolio of sound stocks should expect their prices to fluctuate and should neither be concerned by sizeable declines nor become excited by sizeable advances.' In other words, ignore Mr Market.

Warren Buffett sums it up this way: 'As Benjamin Graham writes, the market is there to serve us, not to instruct us. It just tells us prices. If something is out of line then you can do something about it. It's how you handle that piece of information; how you play out your hand; and letting the market serve you rather than instruct you. Apply those principles and you can't miss.'

Benjamin Graham's advice is that although it is ideal to buy shares when the market is low, it's not wise to wait only for such times. Better, he says, to buy whenever you have spare cash available, *except* during times when the level of prices is above what can be justified 'by well established standards of value'. Even then, said Graham 'there are always bargain opportunities in individual securities'.

Being aware of the craziness of Mr Market, and knowing how to use his mood swings to advantage, is critical for superior performance. The trick, as Warren Buffett has shown over and again, is to keep your head when Mr Market is causing others to lose theirs. To be greedy when everyone else is fearful, and fearful when they are greedy.

# Fisher and Munger – Buffett's Other Major Influencers

*Phil Fisher, the investment scientist*

Warren Buffett says his investment strategy is 85 per cent Benjamin Graham and 15 per cent Phil Fisher, a rather different type of investor. Fisher is another of the investment world's great influencers. Philip A Fisher was from California, a relaxed, different environment to the stuffy East, where Graham came from. He also had a very different approach towards investing.

Once you've read *The Intelligent Investor*, download Phil Fisher's *Common Stocks and Uncommon Profits*. It is especially appealing to those who like to tick all the boxes before buying a share – and there's nothing wrong with that. The book provides more than a dozen questions to ask.

Fisher's 1958 book is regarded as one of the great contributions to the science of investing. For many, it's right up there with *The Intelligent Investor*. Like Graham's masterpiece, it has two cornerstones. Fisher's '15 Points' detail the questions to ask before buying a share. The other rock is the short chapter on 'scuttlebutt' – the informal grapevine.

## Listening to the scuttlebutt

The word 'scuttlebutt' comes from the equivalent of the modern water cooler aboard old-time sailing ships – a bucket around which sailors would gather to rehydrate and gossip. Fisher ascribed his greatest investment successes to the process of successfully interpreting the scuttlebutt around the companies he was researching.

He encouraged his readers to listen closely to scuttlebutt by talking to a business's suppliers, customers, competitors, low-level employees and former staff – anyone who might have a real feel for the company. Scuttlebutt is something we all know but probably haven't thought much about. Scuttlebutt is what your competitors think about you, what your staff think about you, what your suppliers think about you, and what your bankers are thinking about you.

All of us have the ability to understand or to pick up scuttlebutt just by asking the right questions. Fisher warned that, to be valuable, scuttlebutt required the imparter to have total confidence that they would never be quoted, and for the one receiving the information to inquire from numerous sources. Fisher also put great store in tapping into the knowledge of trade association executives, invaluable sources in building his 360-degree appreciation of what was really going on in a business.

## Use scuttlebutt when hiring, too

I have used a variation of scuttlebutt for years when considering new employees. Each newcomer has been required to go through a series of interviews with existing staffers drawn from all levels of the company. It's amazing how even the most focused prospective employee will react differently to those eliciting scuttlebutt about them.

It's an approach that has saved us the heartache that comes from mistakenly hiring someone whose best attribute is an ability to perform brilliantly in an interview. For this approach to work properly, those doing the interviews must themselves be engaged and curious. This is an attribute the most successful of our species not only cultivate in themselves but also work at developing in those around them. What is a visionary other than someone who has refined their curiosity to a fine art?

Phil Fisher believed that you should look at the investable company's management, the kind of business, what's going on inside it and other qualitative stuff. In other words, quantitative is all to do with numbers; qualitative has to do with people. How good are the people? How good is the industry they're in?

## Charlie Munger, the 'book with ears'

Warren Buffett's business partner for more than half a century, and deputy chairman of Berkshire Hathaway, is Charlie Munger, whose investment philosophy is much closer to Fisher than Graham.

Munger grew up 'a few hundred feet' from where Buffett now lives in Farnham Street, Omaha, and, like the Oracle, also worked for pocket money in Buffett's grandfather's grocery store. But because there is seven years between them, it was not until 1959 (when Warren was 28 and Charlie 35) that the two met. As Buffett describes it, 'The Omaha doctor who introduced us predicted that we would hit it off – and we did.'

Buffett describes Munger as possessing 'a wide-ranging brilliance, a prodigious memory and some firm opinions'. He adds: 'I'm not exactly wishy-washy myself, and we sometimes don't agree. In 56 years, however, we've never had an argument. When we differ, Charlie usually ends the conversation by saying: "Warren, think it over and you'll agree with me because you're smart and I'm right."'

Described by his family as a 'book with ears', Charlie is a man of few words. During the five and a half hours he and Warren answer questions during the Berkshire AGM, Munger often confines his comments to a brisk 'I have nothing to add'. Occasionally he throws in some recommended reading. That's the time to take notes.

In one of those brilliant one-liners that makes him such a favourite with the Berkshire faithful, Charlie Munger once quipped that we can learn a lot more from dead people than most of those who are alive. He wasn't being cynical. In his inimitable manner, Warren Buffett's 'senior partner' was trying to urge his audience to learn from the great minds of history.

Munger is especially partial to the ideas of Marcus Aurelius. Studying the emperor's celebrated *Meditations* will help anyone see why Charlie admires this philosopher and general so much.

His suggested reading list has been responsible for my devouring biographies of the American polymath Benjamin Franklin, the work of brilliant behavioural psychologist Robert Cialdini, the philosophy of Marcus Aurelius and, of course, Phil Fisher's *Common Stocks and Uncommon Profits* – the book Charlie introduced to Buffett, changing his investment approach forever.

If you were to find the greatest single influence that Munger has had over Buffett, it was his ability to move him away from cigar butts to being prepared to pay up for a good business. Buffett explains how this happened in the 2014 annual report, in which the two of them also provide their insights into how Berkshire has developed over the past 50 years and what they expect in the years ahead. Download the report from the internet – it is a masterclass in investing and common sense.

But Munger is so much more than Buffett's investment advisor. He has also taught his friend much about life. When asked at a recent Berkshire AGM how to set yourself up for the future, Munger answered: 'Make yourself a very reliable person and stay reliable all your life and it will be difficult for you to fail in whatever you decide to do. I assign the best hour of every day to myself and the world can have the rest. It's worked well for me.' As it will for you.

# The Berkshire Hathaway Story

In 1956, Warren Buffett's idol and boss, Benjamin Graham, decided to retire. Graham had become bored with investing, having beaten the market by an average of 2.5 percentage points for the previous two decades. He wanted to move to the West Coast and indulge himself in his other interests. He was 62. He lectured at UCLA's business school, and spent time at his homes in California and France.

Buffett was offered a partnership at Graham Newman, but without his mentor, he decided, the firm wouldn't be the same. So together with his wife, Susie, and their young family, the Buffetts moved for the last time, leaving New York City for Omaha.

Back home in Nebraska, Buffett brought seven people into his first business, primarily family and friends. They put together $105 000 and created the first Buffett Partnership. He offered them a six per cent guaranteed return per year. Inflation was very low in those days – small single figures. Buffett kept 25 per cent of the profit thereafter.

Looking back, Buffett recalled: 'On 4 May 1956, I started the first partnership. If I were to do the same again, I would do something very similar. You don't need tons of good ideas in this business, just a good idea that is worth a ton. I would be looking around the world for something that was very mispriced and which I understood.'

In the next 13 years, Buffett achieved annual compound growth of 29 per cent on the portfolios and Omaha was abuzz with talk of this young genius. During that time, his partnerships never lost money in a single year. People started knocking on his door. In 1962, six years after he returned to Omaha, Buffett organised the numerous portfolios into a single partnership.

## The business always wins

Now that he had firepower, Buffett decided to buy shares in a New England textile company, a cigar butt called Berkshire Hathaway. It was an uninspired decision. He's so upset about that he still only calls it Berkshire, never referring to the Hathaway part.

Berkshire Hathaway was a poor investment. For the next 20 years, Buffett kept putting money into it, squeezing it and trying to make a return out of textiles. But textiles in North America after the 1960s was a bad business.

Buffett learnt another good lesson from Berkshire. Great management, but bad economics in the business. Who wins? The business. Great business, but bad management. Who wins? The business. The business always wins.

He says the best business to buy is one that could be run by anyone. In the pre-internet age, their amazing economics made newspapers an example of this. Newspapers generated a lot of cash, which made them attractive to own. Buffett said, 'Buy something that could be run by a village idiot because one day it's possible he will.'

By 1965, the Buffett Partnerships were worth $26 million – big money in that era. They kept accumulating shares in Berkshire Hathaway until the partnerships controlled it. Buffett discovered, very quickly, that he wasn't going to be making a lot of money in textiles.

Very soon thereafter, he bought a company that was to be the real driver of his developing empire, a company called National Indemnity Insurance of Omaha. It was offered to Buffett personally. He says, 'The biggest mistake of my life was that I bought it for Berkshire Hathaway – not for myself.'

He paid $8.6 million. Today, it has a net value of $111 billion.

## Using the 'float'

The important thing about the insurance company was the way it generated what is called 'float'. When we as policyholders buy insurance, we pay upfront. You have an accident, you claim from the float. Buffett loved this business because people would give him money to invest until they had a claim, and only then would he have to return it to them. The trick with insurance is to make an underwriting profit, and most of the companies don't achieve that. They make their profit out of using the upfront cash (your premiums, i.e. the float). As those premiums grow, and as the business grows, the float grows as well.

Berkshire's float today is $84 billion. So Warren is able to invest other people's money that they have entrusted to Berkshire's subsidiaries by putting it into their insurance policies. He can allocate that money in any way he chooses and he has done so for many years. That float is never going to leave the business in one fell swoop because the policyholders aren't all going to have an accident on one day.

Buffett's challenge is to use that float efficiently. I don't know if he was a Boy Scout, but he sure knows the Boy Scout's motto because he says, 'You must be prepared'. He does this by keeping lots of cash in his company.

## Cash is like oxygen

By the end of 2014 Berkshire had a share portfolio of $117 billion with another $60 billion in cash on the side. Not because Warren's worried about the stock market but because he says, 'Cash for a company is like oxygen for a human being. You don't notice it until you need it and then it's the only thing that matters.'

The world discovered this during the financial crisis of 2008. The crash had a knock-on effect, making many companies desperate for money. During three weeks in 2009, Buffett applied $16.5 billion of his cash, injecting it into various companies in desperate need. Among them was the Bank of America, which was so strapped for cash it paid him interest and gave him share options on $5 billion worth of its shares at a fixed price. Seven years later, those shares he can buy for $5 billion are worth $12.5 billion. The eventual gain is likely to be higher still, as the option expires only in 2022.

When you have the cash and nobody else has it — that's the time the financial oxygen really works.

## Buying businesses

What Buffett did with the float was not only to buy shares in businesses on the stock market but also to buy businesses in their entirety. This is something he likes to do.

Today, Berkshire has over 80 wholly owned subsidiaries. As we said earlier, ten of those companies would be in the Fortune 500 if they were separately listed. Buffett would say 'ten and a half' because Berkshire owns half of Heinz, which would also be in the Fortune 500.

Over time, Berkshire has become the fifth most valuable company in the world. This is a direct result of Buffett's brilliant asset allocation — the ability of this hard-wired capitalist to put money into the right places.

The most valuable listed company in the world is Apple Inc, which was worth over $700 billion in mid-2015. Then comes Google, at around $450 billion. The next three are pretty close to each other — Microsoft, ExxonMobil and Berkshire.

Berkshire, at number five, started virtually from

scratch in 1965. It shows you what can happen when you back the right entrepreneur at the right time, and what Buffett has achieved through astute investing.

## *What next for Berkshire?*

In one of his letters to shareholders, Buffett wrote about the temperament he is looking for in the person who succeeds him as the custodian of Berkshire's investment portfolio. These are, primarily, independent thinking, emotional stability, a keen understanding of both human and institutional behaviour, and loyalty.

Plus, he added when reflecting on a different question from a shareholder, his successor as Berkshire's Chief Investment Officer will need a deep knowledge of financial history and the ability to identify wealth-threatening risks that have never happened before.

To all intents, Buffett appears to be looking for a younger clone of himself. That's no easy task, especially for the person so identified. Some years back he brought in two managers, Todd Combs and Ted Weschler, who have managed portfolios worth a few billion each. In most years their returns have beaten Buffett's, and as a result their responsibility has been increased.

At pretty much every AGM I've attended since 2005,

at least one of the questions has revolved around what will happen to Berkshire when Buffett dies. The response I like best was from Charlie Munger, who, exasperated at the subject being raised once more, explained that he and Buffett had spent an enormous amount of time making sure the business continues into the future: 'What kind of a man do you think Warren is that he'd leave his legacy to chance?'

# Buying Smart – See's Candy and GEICO

Warren Buffett encapsulates his investment advice this way: 'What you really want is a business that can earn a high Return on Capital Employed and is able to add capital and able to get the same return on the new capital. That perfect investment probably doesn't exist but we keep looking.'

And he's come close. With two amazing businesses that, together with the insurance operations, have been the backbone of the Berkshire business over many years. One is a chocolates-in-the-box operation called See's Candy, which Buffett calls 'a prototype of a dream business'. The other is motor insurance business GEICO, which offers a unique formula of a near-guaranteed return on every new dollar invested in its growth.

## See's Candy

Berkshire bought See's Candy in 1972 for $25 million. At this stage, Warren and Charlie had a company called Blue Chip Stamps. The sellers wanted $30 million. Warren was only prepared to pay $25 million. Charlie tried to get his partner to change his mind, but Warren was determined: 'I'm only paying $25 million.'

Buffett now says that was one of the stupidest things he ever did because, for that extra $5 million, he could have lost out on a business that has generated $1.9 billion in cash flow since 1972 (and into which they've had to invest a mere $40 million). Buffett was lucky. The seller gave in.

The price paid for See's was five times the annual pre-tax profit of $5 million then being generated from sales of $30 million. What made it special, though, was that the business needed just $8 million in capital to conduct its affairs. Using Buffett's Return on Capital Employed ratio translates into See's generating a 62.5 per cent return on capital every year.

That's where the magic begins. The favourable economics flow through to a product sold for cash (which eliminates debtors and the draining impact of bad debts), and as the production and distribution cycle for chocolates is short, there is little cost in holding stocks.

With those kinds of advantages, it shouldn't surprise us that See's Candy has been a highly profitable investment for Berkshire Hathaway. Buffett says: 'Just as Adam and Eve kickstarted an activity that led to seven billion humans, See's has given birth to multiple new streams of cash for us.'

As Buffett is quick to point out, the business is in an unsexy sector – consumption of boxed chocolates in the US is low and growing very slowly. Since 1972, See's production of chocolate has risen at just two per cent a year. But being away from the limelight has the advantage of keeping away new players – enhancing the return for those who stick around.

This kind of business tells us so much about Buffett. What did he do when it was generating all that income? Did he put it back into building more candy stores or expanding the production facilities?

No. That $1.9 billion in cash thrown off by See's Candy was allocated elsewhere in the Berkshire empire. That's similar to the way we should handle our own investment portfolios. When buying different shares, remember that you're investing in a portfolio of businesses. Not pieces of paper.

## GEICO

GEICO is another company that has been a huge success for Buffett.

Buffett coat-tailed his hero Benjamin Graham whenever possible. At 20, while studying under Graham, he went to the library at Columbia University and pulled out *Who's Who*, where he read that Benjamin Graham was the chairman of the board of the Government Employees Insurance Company (GEICO), a direct seller of short-term insurance. If GEICO was good enough for Benjamin Graham to be the chairman of, Buffett wanted to know more.

So one Saturday morning in 1951, he went to Washington, DC, and knocked on the door of the company. The janitor opened. Nobody else seemed to be around, just the janitor.

He said to the janitor, 'I need to talk to somebody. I've come down from New York.' The janitor said, 'Well, there's this guy here called Lorimer Davidson, he's upstairs. He comes in on a Saturday, you might ask him.'

Buffett spent four hours quizzing Lorimer Davidson, who'd come into the office to catch up on some work. He was impressed with the pioneering business model and profit margins that were five times higher than those of other insurers.

For final confirmation, he later asked three of Wall Street's top insurance analysts for their opinion – all of whom said the stock was overpriced.

But, believing in his own research, Buffett invested three-quarters of his total wealth into the company. He also recommended GEICO shares to everyone the stockbroking job brought him into contact with, including a very first sale of stock to his Aunt Alice.

A year later, Buffett cashed in for a 50 per cent profit. But although no longer invested, he always kept a close watch on GEICO.

The diligent Davidson subsequently rose to CEO, and under his stewardship GEICO flourished. But by the early 1970s Davidson had retired and a successor, one Ralph C Peck, had steered the business onto the rocks.

Among Peck's disastrous decisions was chasing premium growth by moving away from the policy of insuring only the best drivers. By 1976, a combination of mushrooming inflation and a surge in claims took GEICO to the brink of bankruptcy, the share price plunging from $42 to $2.

At a heated annual general meeting, Peck was virtually chased out of the building by angry shareholders. A 43-year-old, John J Byrne, was recruited to replace him. But the vultures were circling. Insurance regulators refused to allow GEICO to raise its premiums, but simultaneously demanded that the teetering company find others to reinsure a large part of its business.

## Rescuing GEICO

GEICO would probably have gone bust were it not for Buffett's intervention. By 1976, the young Nebraskan had already established a reputation as a savvy investor.

This was helped by the prescient decision seven years earlier to liquidate all of the Buffett Partnerships. Warren was worried about the level of share prices and, because he couldn't justify valuations ahead of the 1969 crash, effectively closed down his investment business. He took his entire share from the partnerships and invested it in Berkshire, securing control of the company.

With Berkshire, Buffett had wisely invested the money generated by the dying mills. By avoiding the crash and allocating capital sensibly, by 1976 he was sitting on a pile of cash looking for new homes. And he'd never lost his affection for GEICO.

So 25 years after they'd spent that Saturday morning together, he called Davidson to ask for an introduction to GEICO's new CEO. A dinner engagement lasted well into the early hours as Buffett quizzed Byrne on what he intended doing and how he would extract the once-thriving company from the mess.

Satisfied that the problems were the result of a failed strategy, not the business model, Buffett threw himself into supporting the rescue. As he later described it, GEICO wasn't a turnaround. It was a business with a 'localised excisable cancer'.

Buffett piled into the shares and went to work on convincing the regulators to give the business more time. True to his word, new CEO Byrne slashed the staff by half and cancelled hundreds of thousands of loss-making policies. And after being turned down by seven Wall Street firms, the eighth (Salomon Brothers) agreed to underwrite GEICO's capital-raising issue – provided Buffett backed it to the hilt. Which he did.

Six months after struggling to raise the money to keep GEICO afloat, the share price had quadrupled. Unlike his twentysomething self, this time Buffett didn't cash in the profit; instead he continued buying GEICO shares.

By 1980 Berkshire Hathaway owned 33 per cent of the company. The stock was bought at an average price of $6.67 a share. By 1986 the company's annual profit was over $9 a share. Berkshire's share of the company kept rising as GEICO bought back its own shares in the market.

By 1996, Berkshire's stake in GEICO had risen to 50 per cent. It made an offer to other shareholders for the half it didn't own, investing a further $2.3 billion in making the insurer a wholly-owned subsidiary.

GEICO has become one of the brightest jewels in Berkshire's crown, worth over $15 billion. But it was one that could so easily have been lost had Buffett not possessed the courage to risk his reputation and a major slice of capital by making the tough choice, by doing what he knew was right.

# Buffett's Big Four
# Share Investments

Warren Buffett invests only in companies he knows intimately, waits for the right moment and, after he's acquired the position, sits on his hands. He encourages us to follow his example. Nowhere is the wisdom of this approach better illustrated than in the stories behind the way he created the pillars of the Berkshire portfolio, Buffett's 'Big Four' stocks, which account for 60 per cent of the value of the company's $117-billion share portfolio.

The heavy concentration of these Big Four in the Berkshire portfolio illustrates Buffett's view that a smart investor puts all their eggs in one basket but watches the basket very carefully. So when you hear professional investors extolling the virtues of diversification, know that they're hedging their bets. Even the best of them struggle to beat the overall market – like those champions of diversification, the hedge funds.

There's a great deal to learn from the stories of how these stocks became members of Buffett's Big Four. Each of them emphasises the Buffett approach of doing your homework thoroughly and continuously so that when opportunities arise – a 'fat pitch', with a large margin of safety – you're ready and able to pounce.

The Big Four share a number of common characteristics, most obvious of which at the moment is a focus on buying back their own shares when the price falls below intrinsic value. You can almost see Buffett's hand in this approach because, as he explained in the 2014 annual report, repurchasing 'enhances Berkshire's share of future earnings without requiring us to lay out a dime. Their retained earnings also fund business opportunities that usually turn out to be advantageous.' Don't you just love the man's logic?

## *American Express*

The oldest-established member of Buffett's Big Four is American Express, whose moat – its protective advantage, in other words – is a powerful worldwide brand. American Express was founded in 1850 and by the mid-1960s had become the dominant credit card and traveller's cheque issuer in the US. It boasted a proud record of never having missed paying a dividend in 94 years.

Buffett's entry into the stock came as the result of a unique set of circumstances. Among the many Amex assets was a warehouse in Bayonne, New Jersey. This particular warehouse contained huge tanks of vegetable oil, used mainly for salad dressing, and was owned by the self-styled 'Salad Oil King', Anthony de Angelis. Receipts issued by the warehouse were used as collateral for loans.

De Angelis was ambitious. After hearing that the Soviet Union was facing a sunflower crop failure, he hatched a plan to corner the market in soybean oil. But the scheme needed funding. So rather than using the tanks to store actual salad oil, new deliveries consisted of lots of water with only a small layer of oil at the surface to fool the warehouse inspectors.

When De Angelis's scheme went belly-up, the warehouse managers discovered they had issued guarantees worth $150 million on tanks containing mostly seawater. The warehouse and its owner, an Amex subsidiary, filed for bankruptcy.

According to New Jersey law, the parent company was legally entitled to distance itself from the subsidiary. But Amex CEO Howard L Clark (Snr) wouldn't hear of it. Although Amex literally didn't have the $150 million to meet the liability, Clark believed the reputation of a business that issued credit cards and traveller's cheques was all-important.

So instead of walking away, he decided to stand behind the subsidiary, offering the warehouse's creditors $60 million in settlement. A group of shareholders believed Clark was wasting their assets. So they sued their CEO to stop him meeting a liability that could legally be avoided. The company was on the brink. The share price plunged, and Wall Street wondered whether Amex would survive.

While all of this was happening, Warren Buffett, a long-time admirer of the Amex franchise, decided to do his own research. He spent a day at Gorat's, his favourite Omaha steakhouse, sitting behind the cash register chatting to the owner and watching the behaviour of customers. Buffett noticed that, despite the scandal on Wall Street, they kept using their Amex cards as they had always done. He expanded his research into the use of Amex traveller's cheques. The result was identical.

Wall Street might have been panicking, but on Main Street the American Express brand was as strong as ever.

After visiting Clark, the Oracle of Omaha invested almost half of his partnership's capital into American

Express stock, buying five per cent of the company for $13 million. It was a typically courageous act by one whose research and knowledge told him this was a proverbial 'fat pitch' – a term borrowed from baseball parlance.

Buffett reckons these fat pitches come around only once every five years. When they do, you need to recognise them and then have the courage to swing with every ounce of your strength. This is the time, he says, to be really brave.

With so much now at stake, Buffett worked obsessively at helping to pull American Express out of its hole. He testified in the court case that shareholders shouldn't be suing Clark but congratulating him on protecting the group's good name.

The company survived the court action and the Salad Oil Scandal. And after falling to $35, within three years the Amex share price was up almost fivefold. The stock remains one of Berkshire Hathaway's Big Four investments, with Buffett's group now owning 14.8 per cent of the equity.

Berkshire's stake in Amex has grown and by the end of 2014 was worth over $14 billion. That original one-third, bought in 1964 when everyone else was running for cover, has appreciated in value more than a thousandfold. And, as important, laid the foundation for

Buffett's similar acts of corporate bravery in swinging at fat pitches in the years to come.

## *Buying IBM 50 years later*

You've got to love this quote from his 2010 letter to shareholders, in which Buffett wrote: 'I've been reading Annual Reports about IBM for 50 years, but only in March did my thinking crystallise.' IBM is the only one of the Big Four that Berkshire is currently still accumulating in volume, having been its biggest purchase in most years since Buffett started buying the stock.

Buffett absorbs company annual reports with greater relish than most of us consume thrillers. But at a recent Berkshire AGM he revealed that his edge comes from a different process. It's worth visiting here.

When he was a young man, Buffett applied a unique technique when considering a potential investment. Using the coal sector as an example, he said he identified the top ten companies and set up interviews at each of them with the most senior person he could get to. During the discussion, he built a rapport with the executive, asking detailed questions about the business, which showed he had done lots of preparation ahead of the meeting.

Once sufficient trust and respect had been established, Buffett popped the questions that would reveal more than hours of prodding. If the stock market were closed for the next five years, he'd ask, which company in your sector, other than your own, would you be happy to own shares in? And which one's shares would you least like to be holding?

Buffett reckons this technique gave him a unique insight into any industry.

Back to those 50 years of reading IBM annual reports. What was it that finally came together?

As with everything, it's a combination of factors, including intimate knowledge of the business. But perhaps the overriding one in this case was that Buffett loves companies that use excess cash to reinvest in themselves through repurchasing shares at a good price. IBM, by Buffett's estimation, was going to be investing tens of billions over the next five years, using its strong cash flow to enhance shareholder value.

When you see a company aggressively buying back its shares with cash that would otherwise be lying dormant, pay attention. That's the time the 'buy' bells should be ringing in your own ears. When a company buys back shares, it takes them out of the market. After his further purchases of stock in 2014 and the first half of 2015, Berkshire's stake in IBM rose to eight per cent, making it the biggest single shareholder, an investment of over $12 billion.

Interestingly, the average price that Buffett paid for his holding was $170 a share – a 20 per cent premium to the level at which the stock was available in late 2015. Most investors would interpret that as disastrous, given that it translated into a paper loss of almost $2 billion. But for Buffett, a falling share price is a happy event – when you're a long-time buyer you get to accumulate a bigger slice of the company at a cheaper price.

IBM is in an interesting phase of its more than a century of existence. Revenues have been on the slide since 2010, when the company decided to strategically realign its operations, moving focus away from long-standing mainstays such as hardware and semiconductors into new opportunities such as Big Data, security and 'the cloud'. But changing the direction of a super-tanker like IBM takes time, requiring the Buffett-type patience one rarely finds in quarter-to-quarter-obsessed Wall Street.

Although IBM's overall sales have been sliding since the decision was made, a helicopter view reveals strong evidence that the turnaround is working. The revenue contribution from the new target areas, IBM's 'strategic imperatives', has more than doubled since 2010, with annual growth of over 30 per cent being generated in these areas. That's the kind of progress that keeps Buffett buying.

IBM's real achievement, though, has been that, despite lower sales, it has actually grown earnings per share – modestly, perhaps, and mostly aided by the share buy-back (over $100 billion between 2010 and 2013). But it emphasises how the drop in the share price has been the result of Mr Market getting distracted by the top line. Although sales have been sliding, the intrinsic value of the business is improving.

The company gets another tick from Buffett for its strong cash generation, a reflection of the sound under-lying business. Even more so because IBM is buying back shares at prices that are well below their intrinsic value, 'an essential criterion that is often ignored by other management teams', says Buffett.

## Coca-Cola – another investment half a century in gestation

One of the greatest brands in the world is Coca-Cola, which went public in 1919. Recall that Buffett used to buy six-packs of Coke for 25 cents and sell them at five cents each, but he says it wasn't until the summer of 1988 that 'my brain finally established contact with my eyes'.

Until that point he was famously loyal to the rival Pepsi-Cola. But when Coke products replaced the old favourite at the 1988 Berkshire AGM, the 1 000 shareholders who attended that year should have guessed something was afoot. It was only a year later, however, that the real reason for the switch was unveiled to the world.

Buffett has always loved sodas and used to drink a self-made concoction of Pepsi and cherry syrup. In 1987 Don Keough, an old friend who had since become President and Chief Operating Officer of Coca-Cola, introduced Buffett to the newly created Cherry Coke. He was hooked and, in a most unusual act for this devotee of routine, Buffett shocked family and friends by switching his allegiance overnight. But he couldn't bring himself to buy Coca-Cola's shares, fondly known among investors by the stock market symbol KO, as they were just too expensive, offering no margin of safety.

Then came the October 1987 market crash, followed by Coke's entering a price war with Pepsi. The KO quote halved and in some quarters the company was being touted as a possible takeover target. In *The Snowball*, Buffett biographer Alice Schroeder writes: 'The way Warren looked at it, Coca-Cola was no cigar butt, yet it was pouring forth a waterfall of cash and spending only a small portion of that to operate. Since he had studied the company for years, he knew how much money it had made in the past and he could make a sensible judgment of how much Coca-Cola's businesses were going to grow many years into the future.'

Schroeder's description of the thought process is worth repeating as it encapsulates the way Warren Buffett assesses every investment: 'Adding up those estimates of cash flow year after year gave him an ultimate value. Predicting the company's prospects many years from now wasn't a precise science, however. Buffett applied a margin of safety to his estimates. He did this simply by taking a whack at the number, rather than using some complicated model or formula. If the answer didn't hit him over the head like a caveman's club, the investment wasn't worth making.'

He received special dispensation from the stock market authorities not to disclose his trades in Coca-Cola for a year. By the late 1980s, Buffett was so popular among share traders that the mere suggestion he was buying a stock would attract an army of coat-tailers. By the end of 1988, he'd bought six per cent of the company, 14 million shares for $600 million. In March 1989, when his holding was made public, it caused such a rush for KO stock that the New York Stock Exchange had to suspend trading in the shares to prevent the price rocketing out of orbit.

At the instigation of his old pal Don Keough, Buffett was invited onto the board soon after his holding was disclosed, and he has played a key role there in the years since (including being one of two shareholders who instigated the firing of an ineffective CEO). Berkshire is Coca-Cola's biggest shareholder, with ownership of 9.2 per cent. The shares have appreciated twentyfold since Buffett swooped in 1988.

## Wells Fargo

Major US banking group Wells Fargo was another typical Buffett Big Four investment – generated through a fat pitch opportunity.

In 1990, America experienced a banking crisis, caused by the collapse of the savings and loan (S&L) sector. Mr Market panicked, smashing the share price of every banking group, good and bad. Buffett believes that in banks, management ability is amplified because they lend out sometimes up to 20 times their equity. So if the executive team is high class, profits are exaggerated. And vice versa. Tarring all banks with the same brush completely misses this underlying truth.

Buffett had been watching Wells Fargo (established 1852) for many years. So when the chance arose in 1990 to buy a big slug at a great price, he jumped, scooping up the maximum he was allowed under US banking law.

At the 2009 AGM, when the financial world was rocking in the wake of the global financial crisis, Buffett extolled the virtues of Wells Fargo. Prompted by a shareholder asking what was his favourite stock, Buffett replied 'without question – it's Wells Fargo'. He mentioned the company about a dozen times during the seven hours I listened to him during the AGM and press conference that year. On each occasion the reference was favourable.

*'Anytime there is something big and complicated, there is always a chance of mis-pricing.'*

Part of his zeal came from reminding us of the truth that not all banking companies are the same. He repeated that most investors don't take this into account when pricing banking stocks. Wells Fargo shares had followed the sector down, having collapsed from the pre-sub-prime crisis price of $40 to under $10.

Buffett illustrated his point by using the example of two copper mines – one producing at $1 a pound, another at $1.60. Investors, he said, found it easy to understand that at a global copper price of $1.30 the one producer would still do fine while the second would be in deep trouble. But, Buffett said, such stark differences between banking groups were being ignored.

He argued that Wells Fargo ran two mortgage books: one where its own staff wrote the home loans, and the other where the loans were originated through brokers (central characters of the sub-prime disaster). Wells' own book had one-quarter the bad debts of the one written by brokers. Yet investors lumped both together and used the broker-driven result when analysing the numbers.

Charlie Munger offered his support, advising share-holders to study the success of the great entrepreneur Andrew Carnegie, who, in current money terms, built up the second largest fortune of anyone who ever lived (behind John D Rockefeller, Snr). In Munger's thinking: 'The reason Carnegie Steel became the strongest was Carnegie gained his position by investing heavily during every crisis. If you are running your business right, times that look like trouble are the times when you lay the foundations for success. How could it be any different?'

In mid-2009, Buffett rightly predicted Wells Fargo would be one of the major beneficiaries of the financial crisis because of a government-assisted deal to acquire rival Wachovia Bank, which had hit turbulence: 'Wells got a terrific branch network and a huge ($350 billion) deposit base with Wachovia.' That deal gave Wells Fargo a dominant position, one where it now serves one in every three US households – something competition authorities would have blocked in less hectic times.

At the height of the 2009 market meltdown, Buffett was asked by a group of students what to invest in: 'It happened to be a day when Wells Fargo's price dipped below $9 a share. I told them that if I had to put all my net worth into a single share that day, it would be Wells Fargo.' Munger agreed: 'I don't get too excited about these things that occur once every 50 years. Wells Fargo is going to come out of this much stronger.' As you might have expected given the duo's conviction, Wells Fargo's price trebled in the next six years – more than paying the costs for shareholders who made the trip to the AGM that year.

In years to come, Berkshire's Big Four will become the Big Five when Buffett (or his successor) triggers that option on Bank of America stock created in 2011. Berkshire doesn't yet own those BoA shares, but has the right to buy shares worth $12 billion at today's levels at a price of just $5 billion – the legacy of a deal done when the bank desperately needed funding. Like the other four, Bank of America bears witness to Buffett's ability to combine years of research with nerve – enabling him to smash that elusive home run when a fat pitch arrives.

# Buffett's Investment Basics

Spending time as a Buffettologist will soon bring you to the conclusion that, much as Warren gets the plaudits, Berkshire's success is due to a unique double act. Charlie Munger has made a huge contribution to his pal's thinking about investing, and, through him, to ours too.

One of Charlie's favourite credos is 'Invert, always invert ...', an approach he picked up from the nineteenth-century German mathematician and philosopher Carl Jacobi. What Munger means by this is that the best way to do things correctly is to imagine the consequences of acting wrongly. For instance, before buying shares in a company, imagine the worst things that could go wrong. And if it still looks like a bargain, buy big.

One of the best examples I know of the lesson of inversion comes out of South Africa.

During the late 1990s, while the Nasdaq was on a rip and teenagers with a dot.com idea could become instant millionaires, financial madness infected all parts of the planet. A South African serial entrepreneur called Dave King, virtually unknown until that point, was transformed into a local media star by the share price surge of his business, Specialised Outsourcing. Listed at 50 cents a share, a succession of aggressive acquisitions and exciting quarterly forecasts saw the price rise 140-fold in a matter of months.

At the time of this remarkable run, none of the fund managers who had invested in the company's shares was able to explain to me how Specialised Outsourcing actually made its money. And I asked many of them. A number admitted privately that, because it was the 'hot stock' of the moment, unless they owned some their performance relative to competitors would suffer. The shell game ended only when an analyst at Investec, Andrew Cuffe, said the stock was overpriced and questioned its business model. That burst the bubble and not long afterwards the company went into liquidation.

Buffett would never have invested in this house of straw. Or entrusted money to any of the many asset managers who fell over themselves to get a slice of the Specialised Outsourcing action. Because he'd have remembered another of Charlie Munger's chestnuts: 'When a young man comes to sell you something, ask – What do you own and why do you own them? If they can't answer then go somewhere else.' In their haste to get their hands on the hot stock, King's supporters never asked who was selling. Had they done so and realised it was the founder, their ardour would have cooled.

During stock market bubbles, like those when Dave King made his fortune or in the run-up to the crashes of 1969, 1987, 2000 and 2007, becoming a co-owner of the business was the furthest thing from the minds of those buying shares. Unless they'd shown a profit within days, most players dumped their 'underperforming' stock and moved on to the next one. They may as well have been playing numbers on a roulette table. Their results, when the market crashed, showed as much.

As we've seen, Buffett's belief is that private investors have an advantage over professionals – as long as they do their homework. When they do buy, Buffett says, it is done as though the stock market would be closed for the next two or three years. This gives them the security of knowing the operations of the company bought into will keep adding value no matter how the share price might fluctuate: 'It's like looking at buying a farm outside Omaha. You would evaluate the purchase in terms of the return you could get from the farm over time. A daily quotation by some broker would have nothing to do with it. Investment success depends solely on buying into the right business at the right price.'

## The flawed strategy of diversification

Buffett is a long-time critic of the Efficient Market Hypothesis – which holds that share prices fully reflect all available information – and other theories propagated by academics. At another of the AGMs I attended, he reckoned only two things should be taught at business schools: how to value a business, and how to think logically about stock market fluctuations.

Buffett believes it is in the nature of academics that they want to teach students things that *they* know – and that the youngsters don't. This, he feels, introduces a lot of confusing and often erroneous nonsense. Including the widely preached but flawed policy of diversification.

Answering a shareholder who wanted to know whether Buffett would invest 25 per cent of his net worth into a single opportunity, the Oracle of Omaha said: 'There are times when it would be a mistake *not* to have 50 per cent or more in a given situation. There would have been a significant number of times when we'd put 75 per cent of net worth into an investment. You will find opportunities when you put only 20 per cent of your net worth into it, you are short-changing yourself – you should have loaded up.'

In the same conversation Munger added: 'The whole secret of investment is to find situations of non-diversity.

Good professional investors should not practise diversity. That's for the know-nothing investors.' And, they both advise, such amateurs should not even consider individual stocks, but must stick rather to exchange-traded funds (ETFs).

In March 1955, as the pre-eminent expert in the stock market, Benjamin Graham was called before the US Senate's Committee on Banking and Currency to explain whether he was worried about the high level of share prices. It was a lengthy interview, which, as you read through the transcript, suggests the 'know nothing' investors on the committee were trying to get Graham to reveal his supposed secrets.

Typically, Graham stayed away from making any predictions about where share prices were going, explaining that 'I have never specialised in economic forecasting or market forecasting either'. But the really interesting part of the transcript of the hearing comes towards the end when the chairman, Senator JW Fulbright, pressed Graham on why he was confident that the undervalued shares he accumulated would eventually reach their rightful level. In other words, why would the margin of safety be eliminated; why wouldn't the share price always stay depressed?

Graham's response was classic: 'That is one of the mysteries of our business and it is a mystery to me as well as everybody else. We know from experience that eventually the market catches up with value. It realises it in one way or another.'

That is what Warren Buffett believes as well. In 50 years, Buffett has outperformed the S&P 500, the US stock market's overall index, by 34 to 16, or virtually two to one.

On average, in any one year in America, one in three asset managers will outperform the market. And it is not the same ones every year. The impact of Buffett's outperformance is astounding when you add the power of compounded returns – the Eighth Wonder of the World. Had you put $10 000 into the S&P 500 in 1965 – bought the market, in other words – by now you would have trebled your money after adjusting for inflation, ending up with a couple of million. Had that money gone instead into Berkshire, the $10 000 would today be worth $180 million. That shows how Buffett has outperformed, by beating the index two years of every three. That is how he built this incredible business.

## Buffett the frugal

Buffett believes in frugality. Even though he is worth almost $70 billion, Buffett stays in the same house on

Farnham Street he's lived in for decades. It's the same street where his father's stockbroking business was based.

He goes to work seven days a week and preaches an obsessive focus on 'costs, costs, costs'. Investors often forget about the impact of costs. Buffett keeps reminding us. He tells us two things. 'Don't lose money. When you make an investment, don't lose money. Get that margin of safety right and, secondly, don't pay up too much for the transaction.'

In stockbroking, the costs of transacting are often high. Buffett feels so strongly about this that for years he issued a challenge to the hedge fund sector, saying, in essence, 'I'll take $1 million out of my own pocket and put that up against $1 million from anybody. I will back the S&P 500 Index. You can create any portfolio you like. Since I know hedge fund managers charge too much, I believe that I will beat you.'

For years he had no takers. Eventually, in 2007 a company called Protégé Partners put up $1 million. They got lots of publicity and selected the top five hedge funds they could find on Wall Street. Buffett was trying to illustrate why 'know nothing' investors, i.e. the general public, do best by investing in low-cost ETFs that track the index – in this case the S&P 500. His favourite is the Vanguard S&P 500 Tracker, which levies total fees of 0.05 per cent. That's the total/all-in cost.

What happened to his bet? Seven years in and only once – the first year (2008), when the stock market took an awful caning – did the hedge funds outperform the S&P 500. However, in every year since, the market has outperformed the best of Wall Street. Seven years into the bet, Buffett's S&P 500 is +69 per cent and the hedgies are at +19 per cent. The 'know nothings' are killing the 'experts'. Costs are something Buffett urges we pay attention to.

So when you do decide to take the plunge and buy individual shares, what are Buffett's rules?

## Most importantly, a sensible price tag

Never forget the margin of safety. If you're going to buy a share – it can be the greatest company in the world, but if there is no margin of safety, you could lose. This concept is so important that we've devoted an entire chapter to it in this book. Please read it.

## Turn off the stock market

With share price information accessible everywhere, it's hard not to be distracted by market movements.

But Buffett reckons 'turn off the stock market', because a company does not change in value by a few per cent a day in the way the share price suggests it does. A company changes only very slightly in value, and only incrementally.

And if you are going to buy shares, he reckons, you should be prepared to hold on for at least five years. In Berkshire's 2014 annual report, Warren addresses this: 'Since I know of no way to reliably predict market movements, I recommend that you purchase Berkshire shares *only* if you expect to hold them for at least five years. Those who seek short-term profits should look elsewhere.'

Buffett added: 'For those investors who plan to sell within a year or two after their purchase, I can offer no assurances, no matter what the entry price. As Ben Graham said many decades ago, "In the short term the market is a voting machine; in the long run it acts as a weighing machine." Occasionally the voting decisions of investors – amateurs and professionals alike – border on lunacy.'

If you buy any share that you have researched properly at a price that includes a margin of safety, and hold on to it for five years, you have an excellent chance of making a good return on your investment. Anything less than that, the Master tells us, and you are gambling.

So turn off the stock market. Buy the share and forget about it. Time is the friend of a wonderful business and an enemy of the mediocre.

## Look for a business you can understand

So what do you look for when you're buying into a business?

Primarily, a company you can understand. If you're in the tech industry, you might have an advantage over the rest of us. You can perhaps understand Alibaba. Maybe you understand Tencent. Or Facebook. Or Twitter. Maybe you're one of the few human beings who is not linear-processed but knows what exponentiality is about. Perhaps.

Warren Buffett is not one of their number. One of his best friends is Bill Gates, who co-founded Microsoft. They play online bridge once a week. Bill Gates even sits on Berkshire's board. They holiday together and talk often.

So, with all this knowledge, does Buffett own Microsoft shares? No. Of course he understands Microsoft makes software and it's got 'the cloud', et cetera. But for him, actually understanding a business is knowing with a reasonable degree of certainty what the profits will be in the next five years. He can't work that out on Microsoft. So he doesn't own the shares.

## *Buy favourable, long-term economics*

Would I be investing in a motor manufacturer today? Probably not, given the growing threat from driverless cars. Google's driverless cars have done 2.7 million kilometres on California's highways. So far they have had only seven accidents, all of them caused by other drivers.

Would you buy a hotel business today, given the long-term economics of hotels? Not me. The hospitality sector is being disrupted by Airbnb. In five years, it became the most valuable hotel business in the world. The long-term economics of physical hotels are not good. So think about that question carefully. Think about the way things are developing. And taxis? What about the impact of Uber? Or what about network television companies? Netflix is crunching their business models.

In all these and many other examples, the first challenge is to understand the economics of the business. And if you have any doubts of the sustainability, stay away. Nobody forces us to buy a share.

## Able and trustworthy management

Buffett's holding period on shares is 'forever' but he will sell in a flash if it turns out the management are crooks. And he's done it a few times. He did so in 2014 with his holding in UK retailing giant Tesco, which he dumped, taking a $440-million loss. Management there had cooked the books by overstating the value of revenue. That's something Buffett won't forgive.

How do we know the management team is able and trustworthy? It's quite simple – read the annual report. If the report is written by consultants (whose priority is to push the share price), be wary. If the annual report's letter is written by the chairman himself, you can generally trust what he's saying.

Buffett has some suggestions: 'We read a lot about the industry, the competition. We get plenty from reading the annual letters to shareholders. I like the feeling when I'm hearing (in the letter) from somebody who regards me as a partner. If the letter is done by the Investor Relations Department or some consultants, that also tells you a lot. We basically are getting dishonest messages from the management when mistakes are being hidden or not spoken about.'

Buffett believes there are many clues for those needing to uncover dishonesty: 'People give themselves away fairly often. We get suspicious very quickly. We rule out investments 90 per cent the time – and look for the obvious cases of people you can trust.' Adds Munger: 'We're deeply suspicious when the proposition is too good to be true.'

## A company must have an enduring moat

What is a moat? Think about the Middle Ages in Europe, where the nobles would congregate behind high castle walls, and then to make themselves even safer they'd have a moat around the complex.

In the context of capitalism, some companies manage to get governments to protect them for a while. They lobby for import duties or whatever legislative protection might be necessary to support the business. But eventually bad businesses get wiped out. There's no permanent protection from politicians, and companies that do temporarily enjoy protection rarely prosper in the long term.

For a company to flourish, it needs a natural moat. It needs this protection because, in capitalism, if you are making good profits, somebody else is guaranteed to want a bite. Somebody else is always going to want your lunch. So before investing consider whether there's a moat that will protect your company's profit stream.

Most of the companies that Buffett invests in have a moat. Coca-Cola, for instance, has an impregnable global brand. Ditto credit card company American Express. Banking group Wells Fargo possesses a moat in its massive distribution network. Other examples of moats are Google's internet search engine and Apple's computer/phone ecosystem. These are assets that make their profit streams hard for competitors to attack. And that protect your investment too.

## Don't worry about the economy

Sorry for economists, but if you're an investor ignore their forecasts in totality. Do not waste your time reading their economic reports. Too many private investors think they know what the economy is going to do. They scheme it out and then they say, 'Well, this is a sector that is going to be doing well,' and use it as the basis from which to make their purchases. That's flawed logic.

Read Nassim Nicholas Taleb's *Fooled by Randomness* or Daniel Kahneman's *Thinking, Fast and Slow*. They've done research on forecasters over many years. Taleb concludes, 'Better to be lucky than to be skilful, in every instance.' Economists are skilful. They aren't so lucky.

For instance, take 6 December 1941, the day before the Japanese bombed the US Pacific Fleet, changing the course of the Second World War. Who predicted the attack on Pearl Harbor? Or take 8 September 2001: who could have predicted that 9/11 would happen the next day?

We just don't know. Our world has speeded up. We can all make projections and prognostications, but they're usually wrong. As an investor, forget economic forecasts. It is better to buy a business that has the ability to generate profit in any environment. That is all you should be interested in.

## *Buy the business, not the stock*

During most years, Buffett is visited by more than 2 000 students from 35 different universities. He often talks to them about, say, General Motors, and says, 'Don't look at the share price. Don't buy the shares at $30 a share. Ask yourself if you'd buy the company for $50 billion.'

Buffett believes it's a great habit to discipline your-self and treat each purchase as though you were buying the whole company. Then explain to yourself why it would be worth so much and how long it would be before you earned back what you're putting down. This focuses the mind on the true value of the enterprise and stops you getting distracted by a few cents' movement in the share price.

Whether you are buying control of a small business or 100 shares in a large listed company, be sure you understand how it makes its money. You wouldn't hand cash to a stranger, blindly believing he'll increase it for you. So why do something like that when investing in shares? Analysing the numbers is only part of the equation. Understanding what the company actually does is much more important.

Look at what the total company is worth, its market capitalisation, rather than the share price. Should you get confused about these things, just remember that listed shares are merely slices of the business. The company you are thinking of buying into has its ownership cut into tiny portions, so pretty much anyone can afford to be a co-owner.

If you had enough money, you could buy the whole thing. The value of the entire business is its market capitalisation – the number of issued shares multiplied by the current share price. If it gets confusing because the numbers are too big, knock off a few zeroes to make it easier.

Buffett asks: is the business simple and easy to understand? Does it have a consistent operating history? Does it have favourable long-term prospects? Is the management rational and honest? Is management truthful with shareholders? Are the executives driven by fashion, or what we call the institutional imperative?

Simple stuff – buy the business, not the stock.

## Swing at fat pitches

David Shapiro, my stockbroking friend, is a trader. He will see five opportunities in a day and might trade in and out, five minutes here, ten minutes there. A fat pitch is different. It's something really juicy. A long-hop bowled at you in cricket. Or, to use the baseball analogy, the kind of easy throw you should be able to hit out of the ballpark.

Where do you find the 'fat pitch'?

Munger describes waiting for these 'dislocations' as being like a man standing in a stream with a spear waiting for a fish to swim by. It could be a day, a week, a month or even a year before an opportunity presents itself: 'The dislocation is very brief and very extreme: you need to think fast and act decisively.'

In investing, a fat pitch is something you're likely to see only a few times in your life. In Buffett's case, he estimates once every five years. He reckons he's had 12 fat pitches in 50 years at Berkshire. And he says, 'Nowadays, Charlie and I settle for one good idea a year.'

A fat pitch is the dripping roast of investments. When they do come along, take your baseball bat back, swing hard and hit it for all you're worth.

## Stay within your circle of competence

Buffett and Munger put a lot of emphasis on sticking to what they know and actually understand.

Says Buffett: 'Charlie and I have circles of competence that allow us to evaluate certain types of businesses where we can come to judgments that won't change in five or ten years' time. We have three boxes – in, out and too hard. We try to stay in our circles of competence so reject around 90 per cent of the possible investments. As IBM founder Tom Watson (Snr) said, "I'm no genius, but I'm smart in spots and I stay in those spots." We zero in on things we can understand like whether people will be buying more candy in five years' time. We don't play Big Trends – they just don't mean that much. There is too much money to be made year to year rather than waiting for the Big Trends to expose themselves.'

Adds Munger: 'We know the edge of our competency better than most people do. It's not a competency if you don't know the edge of it. When something is too hard to understand, we look for something that is not too hard to do. The trick is getting enough expertise. Most people aren't going to find thousands of things that they are very good at. But they can find one or two things that they really understand.'

Their approach has drawn its share of critics. Like during the 1998-2000 internet bubble, when Buffett was pilloried, accused of having passed his sell-by date. But the duo refuse to be swayed from their simple approach. Says Munger: 'We have failed to profit from one of the biggest commodity booms in history and will probably continue to fail in that way.' But, boy, have they succeeded when operating within their circle of competence.

# Becoming a Superior Investor

In his 2007 letter to shareholders, Buffett writes about the temperament he is looking for in the person who will succeed him as the custodian of Berkshire's investments. These are, primarily: independent thinking, emotional stability, a keen understanding of both human and institutional behaviour, and loyalty. Plus, he added, when reflecting on a different question from a shareholder, his successor as Berkshire's Chief Investment Officer will need a deep knowledge of financial history and the ability to identify wealth-threatening risks that have never happened before.

That sounds like a tall ask. Fear not. Few reading these pages will be expecting to take over a $117-billion share portfolio. The good news is that many of Buffett's principles are common sense. Provided you follow his investment guidelines, anyone with even a sliver of life experience will be able to avoid many of the share market pitfalls.

And the bad news? Well, although the basics are just that, being logical about money has never been easy for mankind. Our thoughts and actions are often hostage to emotion. In the short term, fear and greed often drive markets, pushing the price pendulum far beyond and below true value. Sometimes it can take years before logic reasserts itself. But realising this – and holding your nerve – reaps serious dividends.

*Munger: 'Modern portfolio theory is so asinine.'*

Some of the best advice picked up from studying Warren Buffett is his belief that there is no real difference between buying a business outright and acquiring shares in a company listed on the stock exchange. In both cases, you need to know exactly what it is that you are getting yourself into. And under.

## Assessing management

I spent a big slice of my career hosting a nightly business radio show, interviewing CEOs and occasionally grilling them on the detail in their financial results. The show was broadcast in prime time just after the stock market had closed for the day. Despite it being an arena in which they would be expected to answer some tough questions, there was never a shortage of potential interviewees.

The programme had established a reputation of being an appointment for the business community, and investor relations consultants would book their clients weeks in advance. So I was taken aback one day when a dear friend, who ran one of the biggest consultancies, confided over lunch.

'I must warn you,' he whispered, 'it's getting harder to get my clients to come onto your radio show. They don't like this habit you have of bringing up what they said in previous interviews. Nobody's perfect, you know.' After his words sank in, so did my gratitude. His complaint confirmed my suspicion that many of those running major corporations are nothing like the business geniuses their spin doctors would have us believe.

So how do you rate the custodian of your investment? Or more to the point, how does Warren Buffett do it?

In the 2014 Berkshire annual report, Buffett shares insights into how his company selects and measures the CEOs of its over 80 wholly owned subsidiaries. The same principles can be applied when assessing leaders of those companies whose shares Buffett has invested into. Because running any business is primarily a job of capital allocation and of surrounding yourself with the best possible people.

Here are some of the attributes Buffett looks for:

- Character is crucial – the CEO must be 'all-in for the company, not himself (or herself, as gender or race should never be the factor determining who should lead)'.

- Neither ego nor avarice should motivate him to demand pay that matches those of his peers, even if his accomplishments exceed theirs.

- A CEO's behaviour has a huge matching impact on managers down the line: if shareholders' interests are paramount to him, those down the chain will embrace that way of thinking. And vice versa.

- Good CEOs are in an ongoing battle to fight off the ABCs of business decay: arrogance, bureaucracy and complacency. Buffett says, 'When these corporate cancers metastasise, even the strongest of companies can falter'.

- The stewardship of managers must be trusted, but no matter how strong the values, the CEO must impose an active audit function – 'no sense in being a dammed fool'. In general, though, trust produces better results than 'streams of directives, endless reviews and layers of bureaucracy'.

As a broad guideline, then, managers are custodians of the business for the owners (shareholders) rather than generating the maximum returns for themselves. The other critical assessment is the numbers.

You need to be satisfied that the team is actually adding value to the operation, and not merely going through the motions. This will be reflected in achieving better returns than the competitors, in showing that they are able to reinvest the profits effectively, and in acting in a way that ensures the long-term growth prospects of the business will be achieved.

So what should you look for? Says Buffett: 'A good CEO knows how to make deals. But he also knows how to avoid some types of deals, which is probably more important. It's hard to overemphasise the importance of who is CEO of a company. It's difficult to overpay the truly extraordinary CEO of a giant enterprise. But this species is rare.'

Warren Buffett cautions, again, that you need to be sure that if high margins are being generated by the company, that this comes from having a good management team – not because they own state-issued licences or other unfair advantages. It all boils down to their ability to allocate efficiently whatever resources they have at their disposal.

Some of the biggest businesses are run by the most

wasteful individuals, and some of the smallest by the most enterprising. It is in the natural way of things that over time these realities are reflected in the returns achieved for shareholders. As the shifts come gradually, they can be imperceptible to all but the closest and most patient observer. But shift they do.

The market also gets the relative ability of management wrong. Often. One of the most spectacular examples was the technology group Dimension Data (DiData), a South African-founded company whose global operations were exposed to the world through a London Stock Exchange listing in 2000.

Since its founding in 1984, the company seemed unable to do wrong. Stock-based acquisitions everywhere from Asia to North America seemed inspired by genius as the company cashed in on its inflated share price and the developing tech market. Eventually, its once-humble managers started to believe their own press. Respected investment analysts also ignored danger signs that flashed loud and red for some time before the collapse.

The company had a tradition of inviting its suppliers, friends and the media to a dinner following the publication of its financial year-end results. This event grew from a few close associates to literally hundreds, from a restaurant that comfortably seated all the guests to a massive marquee with so many tables that powerful PA speakers were required to ensure that all the guests could hear the self-congratulatory diatribes.

At one of the last of these year-end jamborees, I asked quite innocently whether the others at our table believed DiData's 30 per cent profit growth rate could be sustained. Such was the attack from the assembled, including one of the directors, that it wouldn't have been worse had I insulted the CEO's wife. The shell game, it appeared, had become a permanent fixture. I was dropped entirely from the guest list after publicly questioning why the company's directors were converting share options and selling them in the millions. There was little satisfaction in watching as the £10 stock price retraced all the way back to below 20 pence as reality finally set in.

The lessons to be drawn from the DiData disaster are detailed in *Who Moved My Share Price?*, a superb little book written by independent consultant Ted Black and business school dean Andy Andrews. Black and his son (real names omitted, of course) play the proverbial observers who wonder out loud about the emperor who was starkers. That the book is written from actual experiences they had with a dismissive DiData management makes the message all the more powerful.

At its core, Black and Andrews' thesis is that management's hot air and hype can fool many people, but the numbers never lie. And they focus on using a model that measures Return on Assets Managed (ROAM) and in particular, Asset Turnover (ATO). By tracking the deterioration in these ratios, they saw that the DiData of the late 1990s was an accident waiting to happen. The authors detail three critical reasons why DiData collapsed so spectacularly. They are well worth repeating and making a note of for future reference. To quote Black and Andrews:

- Firstly, in every business failure of the last 30 years anywhere in the world, you will find that the board of directors was the last to realise that things were going badly wrong. It's a rarely appreciated reality that the board actually only knows what management chooses to tell them. And when everyone is enjoying the benefits, it takes a brave non-executive to ask the difficult questions.

- Secondly, their managers did not know their *only* legitimate purpose was to *maximise the value of the firm* for shareholders. Too often the executives run the business for their own ends, forgetting that they are mere custodians of other people's investments and ownership.

- Thirdly, they were unaware that value derives fundamentally from sustainable productivity of the firm's asset base, not the productivity of its people. It is all too easy to get these concepts confused by emotive characteristics, such as loyalty to staff and the reliance on the 'feel-good' factor that happy workplaces engender. But a business, in the final analysis, will flourish or fall on the quality of its capital allocation – the way the custodians (management) apply the resources at their disposal.

# The Rarest Event – Buffett Calls the Market

Warren Buffett is the epitome of a bottom-up investor. He studies companies and bets on businesses, steering away from 'big picture' scenarios. Buffett refuses to call markets. Well, most of the time. The exceptions are so rare they're worth revisiting.

The most recent of these was on 16 October 2008 when he wrote an opinion piece for the *New York Times* titled 'Buy American. I Am.' The value of US shares had dropped more than 40 per cent in the previous 12 months and the then 78-year-old Buffett believed the mood was so bad he needed to offer some perspective.

*Munger: 'It's a good habit to trumpet your failures and be quiet about your successes.'*

As one with a belief in trumpeting his failures and whispering his triumphs, Buffett would never remind us of that op-ed. Nor of his pre-crash warning about derivatives becoming 'financial weapons of mass destruction.' Or, indeed, those other rare occasions when he just felt he had to go public – and was mostly ignored or written off as a has-been.

In that October 2008 editorial, which proved amazingly prescient (again), Buffett contradicted hordes of pundits predicting a 1930s-type Depression. That alone makes it worth digging it out of the archives. But what made those of us who follow the man closely take notice was because it was also so terribly un-Buffett. This was only the third time he'd spoken publicly about his view on the level of stock markets.

The first time was in 1969, when Buffett liquidated the share-owning partnership he managed because he believed stock market valuations were excessive. The next time was 30 years later when, in July 1999, he threw a lead balloon onto the internet party. This was in his famous closing address at the annual five-day Sun Valley gathering for, mainly, the entrepreneurial, private equity and investment banking leaders of the tech world.

Buffett wasn't well enough known in 1969 for his publicly expressed concerns to register on many radars. But he proved to be spectacularly correct. The US stock market's Dow Jones Industrial Average ended 1969 at 877 points. It was still trading at the same level some 13 years later (1982: 884 points).

Thirty years on, his second pronouncement on markets created a much bigger stir. Alice Schroeder's widely acclaimed biography, *The Snowball*, devotes Chapter Two to Buffett's attempt to single-handedly prick the internet bubble.

Despite a well-reasoned attack on internet stock prices, Buffett's warnings were written off as the last roar of an old lion who 'didn't get the new paradigm'. Even some of his friends believed it was Buffett's way of trying to rationalise how he had missed out on one of the biggest booms in investment history.

For some months after the Sun Valley speech, his critics were able to chuckle about the old man from Omaha as they celebrated the tech-heavy Nasdaq index doubling yet again from July 1999's 2 200 to the ultimate top of 5 048 on 10 March 2000.

The day the Nasdaq peaked, CNN's market roundup typified the mood: 'The divergence between the blue chips and technology is symbolic: The Nasdaq finished above the key 5 000 mark, while the Dow ended below 10 000. Analysts see the trend continuing,' the news channel reported.

It quoted one Donald Selkin, chief investment strategist at brokerage Joseph Gunnar, who opined: 'The Dow would do well to get back to its all-time high while the Nasdaq is in uncharted territory. The Dow has too many stocks whose time has passed.'

Selkin was merely a voice in the crowd of now long-forgotten Buffett sceptics. Their self-delusion led to ill-founded advice that cost clients massively in the months that followed. By late 2002, the Nasdaq Composite index had fallen to a third of the level it had traded at when Buffett issued his much-maligned warning. It lost an astonishing 84 per cent from the peak, with hundreds of once high-flying internet companies disappearing into bankruptcy.

Although it is at the other end of the investment spectrum, Buffett's 2008 call to 'buy American stocks' came out of the blue, pretty much like his previous public forays. He finds forecasting big trends especially distasteful, sticking to his own advice of operating within a 'circle of competence' – occasionally quoting former IBM chairman Tom Watson's credo that you only benefit from being good in patches by sticking to those patches.

*'We don't play trends – they just don't mean that much. There is too much money to be made year to year rather than waiting for the big trends to impose themselves.'*

As with the 1999 Sun Valley speech, Buffett's message in the *New York Times* was logical, clear and drew on his encyclopaedic knowledge of economic history. This time he used examples from the Great Depression, the Second World War and the inflation-ravaged 1980s to show that stock markets anticipate the economy, turning upwards some months before the real world hits its trough.

Buffett stressed that although he believed October 2008 was a great time to buy – and said he was switching his own personal cash from bonds to shares as rapidly as possible – this was not a prediction that stock market prices had necessarily bottomed.

He said the financial world was in a mess and problems leaking into the general economy 'are now turning into a gusher – unemployment will rise, business activity will falter and headlines will continue to be scary.'

But where he differed from the mainstream was a conviction that these were exactly the times when investors should be buying shares: 'Bad news is an investor's best friend.' In his *New York Times* op-ed, he went on: 'A simple rule dictates my buying: Be fearful when others are greedy and be greedy when others are fearful. And most certainly, fear is now widespread, gripping even seasoned investors.'

Those who lose money in shares, he adds, are people who buy only when they 'felt comfort in doing so and then proceeded to sell when the headlines made them queasy. Today, people who hold cash equivalents feel comfortable. They shouldn't. They have opted for a terrible long-term asset, one that pays virtually nothing and is certain to depreciate in value.'

As he had been in 1969 and 1999, Buffett was once again correct in 2008 – and he was ridiculed for it. A year later the market had recovered 20 per cent. Five years after his op-ed, share prices were at double 2008's level. The next time Warren Buffett puts up his hand, it's best that we listen.

# Katharine Graham and
# the Media Business

One of my biggest decisions before starting my second company, Aurelius Media (what else?) and its flagship, BizNews.com, was whether actually to stay in the media industry. With all the disruption being wrought in this sector, there are many easier ways to make a living. But in the end I stuck with what I knew best.

Interestingly, Warren Buffett himself is a long-time fan of the media sector. For him it started in 1971 after a family-owned newspaper business, the *Washington Post*, faced a cash crunch. The crisis came in the wake of the suicide of Phil Graham, its brilliant but unstable CEO. To survive, the company needed to raise money, and did so by listing its shares on the New York Stock Exchange.

Two years after listing, the *Washington Post*'s newly installed CEO and widowed major shareholder, Katharine Graham, discovered that Berkshire had quietly bought 10 per cent of the shares. Worried that Buffett was about to launch a hostile takeover bid, she invited him to Washington to try to dissuade him.

What was to become one of the deepest friendships in both of their lives began inauspiciously. As Buffett arrived at the Washington hotel opposite the Post's offices, the newspaper's unions went on a violent wildcat strike, causing a ruckus clearly visible from the Omaha resident's room.

At a boardroom lunch the next day, one of the embattled Kay Graham's managers attempted to rub in her managerial inadequacies, belittling her by asking a technical financial question about which the recently transplanted housewife obviously had no clue. Buffett rode to Kay's rescue, interrupting with a detailed answer. When he had finished Kay simply added: 'Exactly'. She had found her business hero.

Kay Graham wrote in her subsequent autobiography, *Personal History*, that, when they were alone, Buffett sensed the *Washington Post* owner's concerns about his share purchases. He offered to stop buying shares if that would make her more comfortable. She asked him to – a request that was to cost Buffett a fortune. His initial $10-million investment surged to become worth hundreds of millions as his inputs and Graham's grit turned the *Washington Post* into one of the world's great newspaper companies.

But the opportunity cost was offset by the gain of a friendship that lasted right to the last breath of the gracious lady's eventful life. Buffett was with her at the annual media conference in Sun Valley, Idaho in 2001 when the 84-year-old Graham slipped and fell, hitting her head, dying shortly thereafter.

The way Buffett went about helping Kay Graham to educate herself in the ways of business can serve as an excellent blueprint for anyone wanting to understand this field. Here are the major pointers that Graham shared through her book:

- Buffett put as many annual reports as he could carry under his arm and took Kay through them, describing the different businesses and noting why one business was good and another not. This taught her the specifics while also imparting a great deal of his philosophy.

- With the same zeal that some gather antiques, so Buffett collects 'antique financial statements'. Just as with geography or humans, it is interesting to take a snapshot of a business at widely different points in time – and reflect on what factors produced change as well as what differentiated its specific pattern of development from others also observed.

■ Kay to Warren: 'Your intensity, concentration and drive almost scare me, but are happily relieved by those other things you possess – decency, gaiety, enjoyment and warmth. The long hours of talk started so many new trains of thought, altered some I already had and redirected others.'

■ Kay on Buffett: 'Warren is only happy when he is unconstrained, totally in control of his own life; not forced to go to meetings or dinners he doesn't want to go to or see people who don't interest him or do things he doesn't enjoy. He never calmed me down by false optimism but, rather, by shedding light of reality as he saw it on whatever it was that was haunting me.'

Here are a few nuggets from Buffett and Munger about the media industry.

## On the media business:

'Very few businesses get better because of more competition. The economics of media businesses do not have a great outlook. A media licence used to be a royalty stream generating huge amounts of money. In the past there were, say, three highways between P&G [Procter & Gamble] and the public. But as you build more highways, you decrease the value of these highways. And many more have been built.'

'People are always going to want to be entertained or informed. But each of us has only two eyeballs. As years have gone by we have been informed faster and been entertained in more forms. But what hasn't expanded is the time we have for entertainment or to be informed. The economics have deteriorated for newspapers. Same for TV. The audience keeps going down. In the mid-1980s, *World Book* encyclopaedias sold 300 000 books a year. The problem came when a good alternative arrived in the internet. It isn't that the *World Book* product deteriorated. And this trend won't stop. There are the same pricing events – the value gets extracted in a much different way. It will be a rare business in media that doesn't have a way worse future than its past.'

## On the newspaper industry:

'What multiple should you pay for a business whose earnings are going to fall five per cent a year? We face the prospect of newspaper earnings eroding. I do not think the circulation of our newspapers will be higher in five years or the advertising revenue greater. There's another problem that the perception by those inside the companies is different. People in the business always seem to think they have seen the first rebound. It's been an interesting thing to me to see owners and people in the business resist the reality.'

'When they take people to the cemetery they are burying newspaper readers. They are not being replaced by college graduates. Charlie and I couldn't live without newspapers. But lots of people can. We loved them as products. But we were wrong about their bullet-proof franchise and we have got to believe our eyes what we see in that world. I don't think that anyone has watched the newspaper business more closely than Charlie and I have. It was easily understood 30, 40 years ago if you had an idiot nephew he could have made money out of running a newspaper. We loved newspapers, especially monopoly newspapers. The economics were so simple. It took us a while to see the changes. The newspaper lost penetration when it became a less efficient way of getting into the house.'

Munger: 'If technology didn't change, newspapers would still have been impregnable. But the technology did change.'

'We have said for many years that newspaper organisations are overpriced because of valuations based on rear-view mirrors and not looking ahead. The woes of the newspaper business are well known. Let's assume Mr Gutenberg decided to become a day trader, so never invented moveable type. Then along came the internet and cable TV. And then along came Johannes Gutenberg the 28th with an invention called newspapers which let us read all about what happened yesterday – do you think anyone would be interested?'

## *On why wealthy people buy newspapers:*

'You get many different motivations for those owning newspapers. Some might be noble; others not so noble. Some don't even know what motivates them. You will see a drift in ownership. Owning a newspaper makes you more important. People pay for importance. They also stick their names on buildings. It's part of the human condition, there's nothing wrong with that. Rupert Murdoch would even acknowledge that some part of what he paid for Dow Jones & Company is non-economic. There are two values in a Dow Jones. Most companies are valued on a discounted cash flow over time. But in others, like newspapers, sports teams and movie studios, there is also a psychological value associated with ego or power. It's the same as if the New

York Yankees were put up for sale – the bids would not be based on economic value.'

Adds Munger: 'In Santa Barbara a woman who got a big divorce settlement bought the local newspaper. Some of the integrity that came from the newspaper business was because of their monopolies. With monopolies you can tell them all to go to Hell. It's one thing to ignore the needs of advertisers when you don't need them. There was more integrity from the working journalist in the world of yesteryear than now. The worse the economics of newspapers, the harder it is to have integrity.'

## On Canadian newspaper tycoon Roy Thomson:

'Roy Thomson went from $1 500 for an advert, figured out what the market would accept and kept on doing it. I met him, went to his office. He was very friendly. He said he worked on 45 per cent pre-tax margins – "above that I feel I might be gouging".'

Adds Munger: 'The Scottish have a reputation for sagacity. Roy Thomson's son saw long before everyone else that the future of newspapers wasn't great. He sold out and invested in the electronic sector and did very well out of it. That's very unusual for a media family.'

# Buffett on Life

For many, the real appeal of Warren Buffett stretches far beyond his sensible, wealth-creating investment advice. Buffett's accessibility, humility and old-fashioned Midwest values make him a role model for millions of people around the world. Part of the man's appeal is his direct, clear thinking – and his refusal to be pigeonholed.

Buffett is a capitalist but also a Democrat; he's frugal but also one of the world's greatest philanthropists; he is intensely focused and goes to the office seven days a week, but keeps a clean diary and never 'works' a day in his life.

For many who attend the Berkshire AGM in Omaha, the highlight is when Warren Buffett and Charlie Munger apply their considerable intellect to the business of life. Over the years, I've found their answers to be logical and consistent. Their rational approach to business and investing switches easily to other aspects of human existence.

Here are some classics on the business of life by the famous investors from Omaha, Nebraska.

## *Best investment you can ever make?*

Buffett's response to a question often asked of him would catch many left-brainers by surprise: 'The most important investment you can make is in yourself. Very few people get anything like their potential horsepower translated into the actual horsepower of their output in life. Potential exceeds realisation for many people.'

At one AGM, Buffett illustrated this by relating a story he often uses when meeting student groups: 'Just imagine you're 16 and I was going to give you a car of your choice today, any car you wanted to pick. But there was one catch. It was the only car you were able to have for the rest of your life. You had to make it last. So how would you treat it?

'Well, of course you'd read the owners' manual about five times before you turn the key in the ignition. You would keep it garaged; any little rust would get taken care of immediately; you'd change the oil twice as often as you were supposed to – because you would know it had to last a lifetime.'

He added: 'Then I tell the students you get one body and one mind. And it's going to have to last you a lifetime so you'd better treat it the same way. You'd better start doing it right now because it doesn't do any good if you start working on it when you are 50 or 60 and the little speck of rust has turned into something big.'

Buffett reckons anything invested in one's mind and body pays off hugely: 'The best asset is your own self. You can become to an enormous degree the person you want to be.'

## How to do it?

Back in the area where his advice is most appreciated, Buffett says he often asks university students to imagine they had the chance to own ten per cent of any of their classmates for the rest of their lives. The most popular choice is not the one with the highest IQ or the best grades but, he says 'the person who is the most effective'.

And: 'The reason people are effective is because other people want to work with them, they want to be around them. There are qualities that an individual picks up – being generous, being on time, not claiming more than you deliver, helping other people – all kinds of qualities that turn other people on. And there are things that turn people off. These are habits you pick up.'

Working on having the right habits, he said, is a great investment.

Charlie Munger: 'I would add to that by teaching them to avoid being manipulated to their disadvantage by vendors and by lepers using the standard tricks of the vendor and the leper. You couldn't start with a better book than Robert Cialdini's *Influence*. He's also got a book called *Yes!* Here's two books that I suggest you add to your list.'

Cialdini is the Professor Emeritus of Psychology and Marketing at Arizona State University. He has spent years researching persuasion techniques, so, in Munger's opinion, his findings provide a forewarned-is-forearmed approach to marketing methods. I met Cialdini during one of his roadshows and instantly saw why Buffett and Munger admire him so much. Humble, articulate and the clearest of thinkers, his books are must-reads.

What makes Cialdini's work special is that he has taken a rational perspective of humanity's iron-age mindset and explained how this creates distortions in the space-age world we now inhabit. Many of our behaviours have been taught through experiences that are no longer relevant – and we need to unlearn behaviours to operate best in today's environment.

## *Tap dancing to work*

Buffett urges us to associate with people who are good for us. And if you find yourself in a position where you're forced to work with people you dislike and don't respect, get out. Soonest. How else, he says, is it possible to tap dance to the office? To get to a place where you love what you do so much that you never work a day in your life?

As he puts it: 'Working for people who churn your stomach is like marrying for money. It's wrong at the best of times, but really crazy if you're already rich.'

Munger uses every opportunity to remind us that for every person who is alive today, there are many who passed before. As he puts it: 'Some of the very best people are dead.' Their lessons have been well documented. So learn from them. Says Munger: 'There is nothing wrong with looking back to our ancestors.'

Look at the people Buffett works with. There's the inimitable Charlie Munger and his big pal and fellow contract bridge fan Bill Gates. And then there's the legendary late Rose Blumkin, the reason why the Berkshire Hathaway Group – 340 000 employees – has a retirement age of 104.

At the age of 103, Rose was driving her little scooter around the carpeting section of her Nebraska Furniture

Mart, the Berkshire subsidiary that is the biggest furniture store in the world. Then she retired and died a year later. In her honour, a sad Buffett lamented that she might still be with us if she hadn't handed in her scooter, and promptly raised Berkshire's official retirement age to 104.

## Read, read, read

Buffett has remained insatiably curious. And satisfies this need by reading. A lot.

At one of the now discontinued press conferences after the Berkshire AGM in Omaha, I got close enough to ask him a couple of questions.

*What kind of books do you read, Warren?*
All kinds, but mostly biographies.

*And how many, say in a day?*
Three. There was a time when I'd read five a day, but now it's three.

He was 79 years old at the time.

# Buffettology

There is so much wisdom packed into Warren Buffett's eight and half decades that no single volume could ever do it justice. I've tried to impart some of it in other chapters in this book. But here, in brief, are some of Buffett's views on a range of subjects – helped, naturally, by the occasional contribution from Charlie Munger.

**Derivatives:**
Buffett and Munger were outspoken on the danger of 'financial weapons of mass destruction' before the sub-prime crisis hit in 2008. They took no pleasure in being harbingers and never stooped to saying 'told you so' in the aftermath. But it is worth recalling what Buffett said in 2007, as the derivatives bubble was inflating to near bursting point:

'There is nothing evil about derivatives themselves. But they usually do them on an expanding basis, introducing more leverage to the system. In the 1930s after the Crash they realised that leverage contributed to the Crash. So leverage was regarded as bad, leverage was not taken very seriously and for decades was a source of little attention.

'The introduction of derivatives has made any regulation of leverage a joke. We may not know where the danger begins and what will make it a super-danger. We saw one example of what can happen under forced sale conditions in 1987. The stop-loss orders in the market during the 1987 crash were like pouring gasoline onto a fire. Here we could have the same thing existing, where fund managers with billions of dollars are reacting to the same stimulants.

'One day you will have a very chaotic situation. I have no idea what will cause this thing, but it will happen. Most of the derivatives industry doesn't even recognise how spooky the problem is. This is going to cause a lot of problems in due course. Eventually it will be a big issue.'

**Using financial advisors:**
'In aggregate, the investment profession does not really add value. The idea that got into the investment field was the more they earned, the more they could charge and the more money they got in. If you know enough

about the person, occasionally you can pick a good invest-ment manager. But you cannot be better off after pay-ing two per cent upfront and 20 per cent of the growth in good years and then have the business fold up in bad years.'

**Contrarianism:**
'Being contrarian has no special value over being a trend follower. You will be correct because the facts are cor-rect. In business and investment decisions, focus down to things that are knowable and important.'

**Reading the market:**
'As Benjamin Graham writes, the market is there to serve us, not to instruct us. It just tells us prices. If something is out of line then you can do something about it. It's how you handle that piece of information, how you play out your hand, and letting the market serve you rather than instruct you – apply those prin-ciples and you can't miss.'

'Investing is seeing out 10, 20 years. You don't get paid for what you're seeing now. Because of this, there have been times when we have been able to buy great businesses at a quarter of what they're worth.'

Says Munger: 'The mathematics of investing were set out by Aesop in 600 BC when he said that a bird in the hand is worth two in the bush. It's all about evaluating the future distribution of cash. We throw almost all of the businesses into the "too hard" box. We have always had a curiosity about things. The biggest thing is to have something in your programme where you don't lose a lot. Avoiding catastrophes is very important.'

## What not to invest in:

'I do not want to buy into a business with a very high labour content and products that can be flown in easily from somewhere else. And I do not want to buy into a business where the competitive position will erode over time.'

## And those to invest in:

'We like best the businesses that have very little capital requirements – they make a far better return on investment.'

## Index funds and professional investors:

'I always recommend index funds for the know-nothing investor. The very low-cost index funds (also known as ETFs) will beat the majority of actively managed unit trusts and professionally managed money. Index funds are going to beat the returns of most investors – but promoting them is contrary to the nature of the self-interest of the financial services industry.'

Munger: 'I think it's even worse that last year's most successful fund attracts massive amounts of money this year. [To journalists] If you want to lose your publication a lot of advertising revenue, publish a list of the returns from funds per dollar per year.'

## Duties of a board of directors:

'There are three critical jobs for any board of directors –
- Appoint the right CEO.
- Keep the CEO under control.
- When significant deals come along, have a balanced discussion about what the economic impact of the deal will be to the company.'

## What makes a good investor?

'Investing is not complicated. You didn't need a high IQ to buy junk bonds in 2002. You just had to have the willingness to buy when everybody else was paralysed for some reason or other. Follow logic rather than emotion.'

## Avoiding losses:

'If you are going to invest for a lifetime, you better have a great sensitivity to what is going to stick a zero into the equation. Doing something that raises the possibility of a zero is crazy.'

## Investing for the long term:

'We are in the business of trying to see what the business will be like in 10, 20 years. If it's too tough we don't make a decision. For instance, we know a lot of things that will happen in technology; we just don't know who the winners are going to be. It's very tough in our view to pick winners. It's much easier when there are big barriers to entry.

*Munger: 'Get to a decision by quickly disposing of the no-brainer decisions.'*

'We don't mind being in mundane businesses. In 1972 we paid $25 million for See's Candy. It has given us back $1.9 billion pre-tax. We haven't forced it back into candy stores. We have used that cash in other places.

'Is it really hard to predict that the biggest brickyard in Texas will be the biggest supplier of bricks in Texas in ten years? In 1890, there were 10 billion bricks produced in the US. There are still 10 billion bricks made every year.'

## Companies that travel well:

'We love the idea about being invested in companies with products that can travel. We think about that all the time. We don't mind having earnings in a company that we think will appreciate over time. But not all products do travel: Coca-Cola travels well; Dr Pepper doesn't.'

## Value investing:

'We think value investing makes sense any place. There is no alternative to value investing – do you go for non-value investing? Tipster investing? Dream investing?

'Our Posco Steel investment came about by me turning the pages of a big book from Citigroup which has around 2 000 pages and a company on every page. I picked out about 20 companies from the pages. The group as a whole was selling at three times earnings. So if you buy 20 of them it's a cinch. Investing is all about value. In the end it is all about investing a dollar today to earn more than a dollar tomorrow.'

## Investing in property:

Buffett: 'Charlie and I have both made small amounts of money out of real estate. It's a big market. If it gets sufficiently out of whack, we could step in.'

Munger: 'We have done better in other fields. Better in buying businesses and marketable securities. We missed the last big opportunity in real estate and would probably miss it again.'

## 'Dealmakers':

'We get approached all the time where a financial investor buys a business and then sells it on. They usually auction it, tell us they want to bring in a "strategic" buyer. The idea that someone who bought something for resale would interest us is strange. We are not buyers of anything that financial buyers are interested in. What we like is a business that is being run like it will continue for 100 years but for one reason or another the owner wants to monetise their stake in the company.'

Munger: 'At Berkshire, we are trying to welcome partners. So many financial helpers in the world today talk about doing deals. We have so many new deal flippers in the game that I don't think there is enough money to go around. In the end, we think that Omaha will do better than Wall Street.'

**Private equity:**

Munger: 'We don't like private equity. In the 1930s, mortgages were granted over property that exceeded their value. I think a similar thing is happening in private equity. It's weird, really weird. Then there's the whole concept of house advantage. In private equity investments the partnerships are taking a cut that's like the take of the croupier in Monte Carlo – only bigger.'

**Acquisitions:**

'When a management proudly acquires another company for stock, the shareholders of the acquirer are concurrently selling part of their interest in everything they own. I have made this deal myself a few times – on balance, I have cost you money. Unlike many business buyers, Berkshire has no exit strategy. We buy to keep.'

### Growing a business:

'Every day, in countless ways, the competitive position of each of our businesses grows either weaker or stronger. If we are delighting customers, eliminating unnecessary costs and improving our products and services, we gain strength. But if we treat customers with indifference or tolerate bloat, our businesses will wither.

'On a daily basis, the effects of our actions are imperceptible; cumulatively, though, their consequences are enormous. When our long-term position improves as a result of these unnoticeable actions, we describe the phenomenon as "widening the moat". Doing that is essential if we are to have the kind of business we want in a decade or two from now. We always hope to earn more money in the short term. But when short term and long term conflict, widening the moat must take precedence.'

### Managing a business:

'In 1965, as a textile business, Berkshire Hathaway was probably worth $2 a share. But we did not buy it only for the basis of the business but for the retained earnings and how they could be used. We have a long culture now of rationality. And talent on the operational side to do intelligent things. We would need somebody who doesn't do dumb things and occasionally does something good. Our system rejects ideas that are not rational.'

**Business location:**

'It's not important where you are based. Ninety-nine per cent of what you do is thinking anyway. The same information is available to everyone. It's just a question of how you process it. We want people living where they THINK best. I would rather have people where the frictional cost of life is low. They have no business paying attention to what stock prices are. They only have to come up with one or two good ideas a year – not every day.'

**Who to deal with:**

'It is very hard to discriminate. Charlie admires Costco probably more than Berkshire. Costco is probably the third largest seller of cigarettes in the US. So should we sell Costco? I'm not sure you can draw the line perfectly. All organisations of any size are doing something you can criticise. *Buffalo News* runs ads for investment products I don't like.'

Munger: 'That said, there were some people that we

wouldn't deal with because of their morals. We did that especially at Salomon. But we were in control there. And in Darfur – the conditions of the abused people are so awful that they defy human cognition. Stay tuned. We'll have more of those issues popping up year after year.'

## Running Berkshire:

'Every manager at BH gets a letter from me once a year. I ask them every couple of years what they would do the next day if something were to happen to them. They give their recommendation of a successor, and I keep those in a drawer. In some cases they are 95 per cent as good, in some cases not. It is hard to replace stars. One of the things we have that's going for us is our people don't leave – they love their businesses.

'Our people have the jobs they want. It is tough to be a number two person in one of our companies as we don't have a retirement policy. Maybe some talented people have wanted to move on, but I'm not aware of it. Overall the system works very well.'

## Charities:

'You should pick whatever gives you the most satisfaction. In the US, for most people it is their church. For others it's their school. I would not feel you have to be as objective about that as I would be with picking equities. With this I would go with my gut.'

## Inflation:

'The best protection for inflation is your own earnings power. The second best is investing in a wonderful business; not a cyclical business like metals, but one that produces sustainable growth. Inflation is bad news for investors – Berkshire Hathaway would not do as well in times of high inflation.'

## Inflation data:

'Core inflation excludes energy and food. To me, these two are pretty core. CPI [the Consumer Price Index] has understated inflation for a great many people – for the person driving to work, cost of living increases have been much higher than CPI. Inflation is very uneven. There have been big adjustments in steel, petrochemicals and others. But the CPI underestimates this adjustment.'

## Gambling:

'Gambling involves creating risk where it doesn't need to be created. The desire for people to gamble has always been with us. The human propensity to gamble is huge. The easier it is made, the more people will do it. I think to quite an extent it is a tax on ignorance. I find it socially distasteful when a government preys on the weaknesses of its citizens. It relieves taxes on those who don't fall for that.'

## Short-selling:

'There's nothing evil about selling things short. It's a tough way to make a living. There are people on the short side who have tried to do things to make stocks go down, some of which is appropriate, some not so. Very often in times when a huge short interest exists there have been frauds or things of that kind. If somebody is running something that is fraudulent, they focus on it full time. But in the long term short funds are unlikely to make money.'

## Charlie Munger's orang-utan theory:

'If a smart person goes into a room with an orang-utan and explains whatever his or her idea is, the orang-utan just sits there and eats his banana, but at the end of the conversation the person doing the explaining comes out smarter.'

## China:

'In 1790, the USA had 4 million people, China had 290 million. Today the US accounts for over 25 per cent of world GDP, China a tenth of that. This has happened not because we Americans are smarter than the Chinese. It's only because our system worked better in terms of delivering goods and services. The Chinese had a system that did not unleash their human potential, one that diminished the potential of their people. And because of the large population they did not use technology. Now they are taking this huge reserve of brains and energy and adopting a better system. There is no reason why they shouldn't have the same positive results as we did.'

## Why is Warren so healthy?

'Never smoked and never drank at all. And I have a job with no stress. When you have these advantages, you can afford to have a bite or two of peanut brittle. A lot is in the genes. So when my mother got to 80, I bought her an exercise bike.'

## Estate duty:

'I don't believe in the divine right of the womb. I believe in equal opportunity. Of the 2 million people who died in the US last year only half may have qualified for estate duty. Around 4 000 had estates of $40 million or more and in these cases the tax should be more aggressive, we should raise the threshold. We don't compete at the

Olympics on heredity. I'd rather that people with talent and hard work succeed than those who were well born.'

**Warren's wedding:**
'Married to a Latvian so had a very small wedding at home. My daughter, wife's sister, two dogs and a cat.'

**The rich getting richer:**
'In my view the super-rich versus the rest has changed dramatically in the last 15 years or so. The tax system has changed. The government has said if you earn your money in any way you are punished. If you earn it from capital gains and dividends you pay very little, around 15 per cent. The super-rich has become a favoured class; their wealth has really gone into the stratosphere.'

**Threats to the world:**
'The ultimate problem the world faces today is the state-sponsored use of terrorism. Since 1945 the potential for inflicting harm on an incredible number of people has risen geometrically. People will justify their use of force if they feel threatened. What has held it in check is the degree to which knowledge and materials are controlled. The genie is out of the bottle. I would like the leaders of the world to recognise it as the number one problem.

The world has become complacent. We could easily have an event that would change people's perceptions in a hurry.'

# My First Berkshire AGM – May 2005

The one-man band would struggle to land a gig in a big city. But the wall-to-wall Berkshire Hathaway pilgrims aren't complaining. Neither are they here for the music. It's Friday night ahead of the world's best-attended annual general meeting. And anyone shoehorned into Gorat's Steakhouse feels privileged. This, after all, is Warren Buffett's favourite eatery. And for this weekend, it's all about Buffett.

Our two-hour interlude between the booked time and when we're finally seated is spent hard up against the small dance floor. Those seats, together with the entertainer's determination to make the most of his one-night-a-year full house, make conversation tricky.

But between songs, the veterans of our party explain how we're not really here for the food. Or the music. Rather, it's to get a feel for what makes Omaha's favourite son tick. It works. For its part, Gorat's décor, entertainment and overwhelmed staff would fit comfortably into the culinary strip of any small town in a remote area.

Gorat's is authentic American Midwest. Right down to the oversized waitresses, hefty steaks, reasonable prices and casual approach to time. Like Buffett himself, it oozes consistency. This is the kind of place where you get precisely what you expect. Surprises are not on the menu.

Travelling to Omaha is not easy. Located almost precisely in the centre of the USA, it's a two-stop journey – and a squeeze into overbooked flights – from most American cities. That turns the trip from Johannesburg into a 30-hour marathon. Once you get there, Omaha has little to recommend it beyond wide roads, clean pavements and plenty of open space. A bit like Australia's Perth without the Swan River.

But it's also home to the world's most successful investor. And when the Oracle of Omaha briefly lifts his veil during the first weekend in May, the investment world's money mountains flock to hear their Mohammed.

Being well primed, this is not a disappointment. Since announcing publicly my decision to join the pilgrimage to the Berkshire Hathaway AGM, Buffett fans have bombarded my mailbox with information. One sent half a dozen DVDs, mostly featuring interviews with the

Oracle. Another, chairman of a major banking group, bought me a copy of Roger Lowenstein's bestseller, *Buffett: The Making of an American Capitalist*, which he reckons is the best of at least a dozen books about the man. He later checked if I'd read it. Buffett followers believe in making proper introductions to their hero.

When Gorat's finally seats us, the steaks ('What does Warren eat – OK, I'll also have the T-bone') are exactly what you'd expect: simply prepared, good-quality meat with a generous strip of fat.

And that's where you start 'getting' the Buffett story in a way no book could explain.

Most middle-class humanity dreams of being able to afford an upgrade from the local McDonald's to the restaurant at the Ritz-Carlton. For them to hear a man who is worth billions say he prefers things the other way around is hard to stomach. So too, in more elevated circles, is Buffett's allegiance to the extreme weather and limited entertainment of Omaha, Nebraska.

But read his story, examine the folksy shareholder letters, watch the DVDs and you'll quickly realise it's Buffett's consistency that makes him such a great investor. He and long-time partner Charlie Munger believe their greatest asset is knowing the limit of their area of competence. They simply ignore stuff they struggle to understand, dispatching it into the 'too hard' category, known elsewhere as File 13.

This ability to keep his feet firmly planted on Mother Earth is probably the most potent weapon in Buffett's investment armoury. Something that becomes obvious the more you learn about the man who prefers his Cherry Coke from the can and whose dietary preferences (steak, burgers, candy) won't make any Heart Foundation manuals.

His humility has a major upside. Virtually everyone I met in Omaha loves Warren Buffett. Taxi drivers boast that he has lived in the same modest home for decades. Early investors and townsfolk say he's a regular guy who drives his own car and eats out where they do. And they praise the generous donations Buffett has made to Omaha schools and other worthy local causes.

The only critics I encountered were a handful of anti-abortion protestors brandishing blown-up pictures of dismembered fetuses. They curse Buffett for supporting family planning clinics. And apparently every year use the opportunity of shivering AGM queues to get their message across.

We joined the chilly lines shortly after 6 am on Saturday morning, guided again by our AGM veteran. Although the doors to the arena opened only at 7.30 (with proceedings starting a full hour later), the old-timer warned that getting there any later could force us into one of the video-only rooms. None of us had come halfway across the world to miss the opportunity of seeing the Warren and Charlie Show in the flesh.

That this was going to be the most unusual AGM of my life was confirmed by the entertainment, which included a smiling cowgirl who rode up to us on a white, saddled longhorn steer. A Texan, complete with Stetson and four-metre stilts, later echoed her 'Howdy' greeting. Both were advertising the wares of a Berkshire subsidiary that specialises in making and selling cowboy boots.

One of the DVDs I watched in preparation for the visit describes the Berkshire AGM as the 'Woodstock of Capitalism'. That's true in a broader sense too.

Apart from the Warren and Charlie Show, Berkshire's subsidiaries use the event as a sales booster, tapping into the wallets of the mostly well-heeled pilgrims who descend on Omaha. During the first Saturday in May, the cavernous basement of the convention centre becomes a place where the group's subsidiaries display 'for sale' wares at specially discounted prices.

When the doors finally open, it feels like every one of those tens of thousands of shareholders is at your shoulder. The tide of humanity jostles its way into the conference centre and there's an impromptu race over the couple of hundred metres for the entrances to the arena proper.

Our AGM veteran leads us around a few corners and up to a block of seats that he assures us will provide an excellent view. Newspapers are rapidly placed over chairs to 'book' places for other members of our party.

Mission accomplished, it's downstairs again to sample the free coffee and pastries from the tables liberally scattered around the arena. I wait out the final hour with another Buffett aficionado, an asset manager who made his first trip six years earlier. He then got a pal in the same business to join him the following year. And he's been coming ever since.

An occasional obligation to sit through corporate videos is one of the few downsides of financial journalism. So my heart sank when the lights of the arena dimmed and Warren Buffett appeared on the big screens explaining that before the much-anticipated question and answer session, it was time for Berkshire Hathaway's traditional 'company movie'.

Buffett must also have watched too much corporate narcissism. Berkshire's version was like, well, a movie. It started with a cartooned Oprah Winfrey 'Omaha Idol', a skit on the popular TV talent show. Except this time it's a competition for Berkshire's money between ideas proposed by IT stars Steve Jobs (Apple) and Bill Gates (Microsoft) and rap artist Snoop Dogg.

In line with the self-deprecating thread of this memorable day, Buffett is the butt of most of the movie's jokes. And, naturally, Snoop's business idea wins the contest against Jobs and Gates. Cameo roles by golfer Tiger Woods, comedian Ellen DeGeneres and Bill and Melinda Gates, among other global personalities, show that affection for Omaha's Oracle stretches far beyond his home town.

The biggest laugh from the packed arena erupts when the movie (produced by his daughter Susie) tracks Buffett phoning Charlie Munger to ask permission to invest heavily into a new discovery he's made – internet shares that Buffett guarantees will be 'hot, hot, hot …'

There follow segments in which Buffett tries to get actress Jamie Lee Curtis to use her charms to bribe his eightysomething partner into changing his mind about the idea. Jamie is not the only one to fall for unlikely Casanova Munger; he is also the prize catch in a segment featuring the five main characters of *Desperate Housewives*.

Apart from the wisecracks, capitalism seeps through the entertaining production. Each segment is interspersed with adverts customised for the AGM by Berkshire subsidiaries. There's also Buffett's upfront disclaimer that shareholders need not worry about the costs as nobody appearing in the movie requested nor was paid a fee (naturally).

The movie provides the ideal warm-up act for the main event, which stretches, in two sessions, for a full five and a half hours. Sustained by Coca-Cola and peanut brittle produced by Berkshire subsidiary See's Candy, their repartee suggests age has sharpened rather than dulled the duo's minds.

They are merciless in flaying vested interests, ranging from investment intermediaries to remuneration consultants. But, by now, research has prepared me for the Berkshire obsession with old-fashioned values, so hearing the don't-give-a-damn trait of pointing and laughing at naked emperors comes as no surprise.

Before launching into the questions, Buffett introduces shareholders to the management team of Berkshire's latest acquisition, its first outside the USA. It involves the $4-billion acquisition of Israeli-headquartered precision tools multinational Iscar Metalworking, a deal announced publicly the day before.

Unusually for the AGM, Iscar's CEO Eitan Wertheimer is handed the floor after Buffett explains that his interest had been aroused the previous October through a page-and-a-half letter of motivation sent from Israel. Wertheimer plays to the crowd, talking the Berkshire talk, generating applause with a quip about his 5 000-person team joining a bigger family.

A ripple of laughter runs through the packed arena when Wertheimer mentions he has been with Iscar for 'only' 34 years. Buffett and his followers love stuff that is built to last. Long relationships are part of the essence of the man and the enterprise he has created.

Not surprisingly in the light of the Iscar move, Berkshire's international ambitions were probed by a number of the fortunate few able to pose questions from 13 microphone posts scattered around the arena and in the adjoining video-only ballrooms. Our group was ensconced just four rows above mic number seven, but with around a dozen people ahead of us in the queue, it was useless to even try and land a blow.

As the discussions progressed, it became increasingly apparent that geographical diversification is a massive step for Buffett, whose love for the familiar is legendary. Indeed, an off-the-cuff line about the cartoon gecko used in adverts by subsidiary GEICO suggested he was confused by the difference between an upper-class English accent and an Australian one.

So his comment about 'doing less directly in currency futures because there are considerably better ways of mitigating the US dollar's decline' suggests more Iscar-type deals could be on the cards.

Buffett and Munger gave little away, but did reveal an even bigger international acquisition was being considered. 'We've got one at the moment which could take as much as $15 billion cash, but it's a low probability. We don't like having excess cash around ($37 billion at end March) but even less doing a dumb deal.'

Part of their problem is that offshore opportunities rarely have the capacity to absorb enough cash to 'move the needle' of the Berkshire operation. Buffett laments that he was 'only able to get $400 million into Petro-China [his best-known foreign investment] and we would have liked to get more'. Turning a couple of billion dollars' profit there surely stimulated his appetite for non-American investments.

Buffett remains scathing as ever about current US economic policies. But he adds a warning about the sheer size of the American economic engine. As Munger puts it: 'We recognise that it [the decline] could take a long time, but it will eventually have to pay.' Buffett added: 'I think you will see consequences at some point, one of them significantly higher inflation,' but with Europe a poor alternative 'it's not totally irrational that investors still like the US despite its faults.'

*'We don't like having excess cash around, but even less doing a dumb deal.'*

So if he's predicting higher US inflation, surely that would mean stronger commodity prices? Unfortunately not, because in Buffett's opinion, commodities have already run too far. He reckons 'the speculators have taken over – what the wise man does in the beginning, the fool does in the end.'

Buffett says the first public AGM, in 1981, was held in a coffee shop in downtown Omaha. It drew an audience of 12, which, he says, included an uncle and an aunt. Buffett is hoping the crowds grow even bigger in years to come, and has even thought about asking local Omaha shareholders to consider giving up their seats to outsiders.

He rejects the idea of webcasting the meeting: 'We could do it but I think there is something to be gained by personal contact. I like the turnout. If we were to webcast the meeting, it would be like turning on a TV show and wouldn't be the same. We want shareholders to have a good time and feel like partners. They're the people putting up the money, the people we work for. They like the feeling of partnership, of being owners of Berkshire with us.'

Anyone visiting Berkyville during that first weekend in May would simply have to agree.

# Questions and Answers

Before we visit some of the questions I'm often asked at my Invest Like Buffett seminars, one of the finest examples Warren Buffett sets for us is to do what you love.

Buffett's not the only one to tell us this. The late Steve Jobs said the same thing in his famous Stanford University 2005 Commencement Address: 'If what you're doing at the moment ... if you look at yourself in the mirror in the morning and say, "If I have to do this for the rest of my life, would I continue doing it?" and the answer is no, look, and if you don't immediately find it, keep looking. As with any affair of the heart, you'll know it when you find it.'

## What are your thoughts on value investing in the era of QE?

Understanding the consequences of quantitative

easing (QE) is outside my circle of competence. QE is unprecedented. Nobody knows what's going to happen as a result. Nobody understands where it's going to end. What I do know is that if there's lots of money in the system – or no money in the system – a company's intrinsic value remains the same. If the price of the company (as pitched by Mr Market) has been pushed into the stratosphere, I'm not interested and neither should you be. QE has pumped money into the system, inflating some share prices artificially. We simply need to stick to the basics – nice and simple.

### How do you work out intrinsic value?

It is something that you will get better at over time, but you can start with tangible net asset value (NAV) as a starting point. A lot of the net asset values that we see need to be interrogated. Banks, for instance, give you two net asset value figures – tangible NAV and the total NAV, which includes goodwill. So be careful. The point is you'll get better at this over time.

The best thing is to focus on the cash flow. Executives can fiddle with a lot of things in the accounts. I've run a public company. I've fought with the auditors. I know what the auditors do and where and when they'll be persuaded to change their minds. I've sat on a couple of other public company boards as well. Usually, the chief executive of the company appoints the auditor. If the chief executive wants a particular thing to happen hard enough, it doesn't mean that he's going to turn the auditor around as happened with Andersen and Enron, but he will be able to influence them. So be careful of bald numbers. You can interpret them in different ways.

Just look at the cash flow. Don't look only at the dividend stream because many great companies, like Berkshire, don't pay dividends. Look at the cash flow in the business, and then be confident the managers are going to use that cash wisely.

Buffett rarely sells, but in 2014 he took a knock of $440 million on London-listed Tesco. He bought into Tesco, the biggest retailer in the UK, because he believed the story they told him. When he discovered the executives hadn't been telling him the truth, he got out. If you find the same thing with any company you invest in ... If you want to invest like Warren Buffett – take your knock.

Fortunately, most companies and company executives are honest. You get better at recognising it with time.

**Last year, when you came back from Omaha, you spoke about *Dream Big* – the story behind the rise of 3G Capital. What is Warren Buffett currently reading and what are you currently reading?**
I don't know what he's reading now. He stopped having

the press conference when he turned 80. Up to that point, I used to crack an invitation as part of the accredited media. About 40 of us would go on a Sunday afternoon to the Marriott Hotel – a very normal place – and we'd each get a chance to ask a question.

Afterwards, you could get close up to Mr Buffett and talk informally. He's stopped that now, so I don't know what he's reading. I can tell you that he told me he's slowed down on his reading. He only reads three books per day!

There's another insightful description on that context in the 2014 annual report, in which Charlie Munger explains what Warren Buffett's successor will need to do. One of the key things is he's going to need to be able to think and read.

I have a big book of all Berkshire's annual reports, going back to when Buffett took control of the company in 1965. They contain some of the most beautiful financial writing you could imagine. Right now I'm reading Daniel Kahneman's *Thinking, Fast and Slow*, alternating with Ashlee Vance's biography of Elon Musk and Robert 'Rich Dad Poor Dad' Kiyosaki's excellent *Second Chance*.

## What was one of the major things at the AGM this year?

I didn't go. I've been going for ten years, a few years on, then one year off. After a while you get an idea of what's going to be said as it's consistent. It's margin of safety. It's 'the biggest investment you'll ever make is the person you marry'. However, with this being the 50th year ... Remember, 39 000 people go to Omaha for the AGM every year, I was expecting a bit of a bunfight. They take the prices of airline tickets and escalate them so rudely that Buffett is now saying to his shareholders, 'Fly not to Omaha, but to Kansas City. Hire a car and drive through for two hours.' We stay in something similar to a Formula 1 hotel. Normal price: $80/night. Berkshire week: $350. I'll go back next year, though.

## How do you apply all of this to your own investing?

Warren says, 'When we buy See's Candy or Coca-Cola we're not going to need a high margin of safety. When we see a great business it's like when someone walks in the door weighing 300 or 325 pounds – you don't need to know exactly what they weigh to know they're fat. If we find something that's a great business we can see it from a long way.'

So don't get confused by the stuff the investment industry tries to confuse you with. It's simple. If you don't understand it, remember: don't buy it.

When you get off the aeroplane at Omaha airport, you see Warren Buffett's picture as a 20-year-old, and it says, 'My advice: invest in yourself.' That's what I do. I invest in BizNews. I invested in my own company.

Investing is not rocket science. It's a combination of knowing what you're buying, understanding that you need to buy in at a good price, and having patience. In the same way as something that you understand very well.

Investing in shares – equities – is a wonderful experience. It's one of the biggest games in the world, and because of stock market regulations the executives are forced to tell us what's going on in their companies. The regulators and the stock exchange authorities force companies to disclose all the facts. If the executives of a company are being devious, it's not difficult to work it out. For instance, if the company is growing by issuing lots of shares to buy other businesses, be wary.

You might want to start by looking at our BizNews portfolio. We have pharmaceutical multinational Novo Nordisk, a fabulous company. Unfortunately, it's gone up 38 per cent since we bought it six months ago, which is a bit of a worry because now you think, 'It was good value then. Is it good value now?'

Go and read about IBM. Berkshire Hathaway itself is a fantastic business with a good margin of safety.

How does the margin of safety work there? They've said they'd be prepared to buy back shares at 120 per cent of the book value. Why? Because the book value understates, hugely, the intrinsic value. Take a company like GEICO; it was put into Berkshire's balance sheet (and book value) at $2 billion and now it is worth $15 billion.

Investing in shares is a wonderful lifelong learning experience that gives you the ability to take responsibility for your own wealth, rather than what our parents did — abdicating that responsibility to someone who's often just looking for the highest commission.

## What happens when Warren Buffett's no longer there?

It's a question asked at every AGM. Charlie Munger says, 'If Warren were to blow his succession, he would have blown his life's work.' Buffett's a man of great intellect. He's a man who plans things well. He's the most rational of human beings. His succession has been well planned. They have a person who will take over as CEO if he were to die tomorrow.

Warren wants his son Howard to become the next chairman. Mostly because Howard understands his father better than most, which is not surprising. In addition, Howard will be able to stop any chief executive who gets out of line. That's the most difficult job. Buffett says there are two big things that a board of directors has to do. Firstly, appoint the chief executive, and secondly, make sure that the chief executive does not become full of hubris.

He talks about the bad ABC of business: arrogance, bureaucracy and complacency. Berkshire Hathaway has 340 000 employees. The head office has 25 people. No arrogance, no complacency and no bureaucracy. Buffett wants it to stay that way after he's gone.

If you read through the work done on that subject, the Berkshire succession is pretty well looked after. Interestingly, on that, Buffett gives an annual dinner, for which people bid for tickets, with the money raised going to a charity. When they first started the dinner, people had to send in their bids via the post, and in the first few years the event raised $25 000. Then the auction went online and became a big competition. The most recent guy, in 2015, paid over $3 million for the privilege of having dinner with Buffett.

In 2010 and 2011, a gentleman by the name of Ted Weschler won it twice by bidding $2.6 million each year. He's an investment manager. Those two dinners got him a job. He now works for Warren Buffett as one of Berkshire's two portfolio managers – Todd Combs is the other – who, when Buffett finally leaves or dies, will run that $117-billion share portfolio. Ted made a pretty good investment, didn't he?

## What is your view about using technical analysis to analyse companies?

I will not dignify that with an answer. Just kidding. Long-term charts help us to see whether the share price is at a level where it offers value. But that's it. I wouldn't buy or sell a share because of so-called technical analysis signals. That's for traders, for speculators. Not for investors.

## When does Buffett sell?

Firstly, when the management is dishonest or economical with the truth. He will get out and he would tell all of us. As he did with Tesco.

Remember, when you buy shares, you're buying a portfolio of businesses. If you own five shares and the fat pitch arrives, you don't say, 'Oh, I have these five shares. I can't do anything with them so I don't have money to hit the fat pitch.'

You reassess your investment and reallocate to the fat pitch. Buffett's view is that if you hold a share for five years you will make money. In between those five years, it's very possible that something better will come along. It does happen, and if something better comes along there's nothing to say holding on for at least five years is the Holy Grail.

Buffett's done it himself. He will lighten his holdings in some stocks to buy better ones. Although in his Big Four – Amex, Coca-Cola, IBM and Wells Fargo – he won't touch them. That's what we all have to try to get, our own Big Four, companies you know intimately, companies you hold forever and buy more of when they become cheap again.

# Recommended Reading

'Read everything you can. I don't think there is anything like reading,' says Buffett, who by the age of ten had read (and often reread) every book about investing in Omaha's Public Library.

He said Benjamin Graham's *The Intelligent Investor*, which he first read at age 19, created a framework that he keeps adding to virtually every day, more than 60 years later.

Buffett reckons: 'Read, and then on a small scale, do something yourself. Once you've done your reading, you need to jump in the water. Investing on paper and investing with money is a bit like reading a romance novel and doing something about it.'

Here are some recommendations to get you started. All of these are available from online retailers and good bookshops:

## Investment classics

Philip A Fisher, *Common Stocks and Uncommon Profits and Other Writings*. Wiley Investment Classics. John Wiley & Sons, 1996.

Benjamin Graham, *The Intelligent Investor: The Definitive Book on Value Investing*. Revised edition. HarperBusiness, 2003.

Benjamin Graham with David L Dodd, *Security Analysis*. Sixth edition. Foreword by Warren Buffett. McGraw-Hill Professional, 2008.

## Books about Warren Buffett

Robert G Hagstrom, *The Warren Buffett Way*. Third edition. John Wiley & Sons, 2013.

Carol Loomis, *Tap Dancing to Work: Warren Buffett on Practically Everything, 1966–2013*. Portfolio Penguin, 2014.

Roger Lowenstein, *Buffett: the Making of an American Capitalist*. Orion, 1997.

Robert P Miles, *The Warren Buffett CEO: Secrets from the Berkshire Hathaway Managers*. Wiley, 2003.

Alice Schroeder, *The Snowball: Warren Buffett and the Business of Life*. Bloomsbury Publishing, 2009.

## Berkshire Hathaway

Warren Buffett, *Berkshire Hathaway Letters to Shareholders 1965–2013*. Max Olson, 2013.

Janet Lowe, *Damn Right! Behind the Scenes with Berkshire Hathaway Billionaire Charlie Munger*. Foreword by Warren Buffett. Wiley, 2003.

## Charlie Munger

Peter Bevelin, *Seeking Wisdom: From Darwin to Munger*. Third edition. PCA Publications, 2003.

Peter D Kaufman (editor), *Poor Charlie's Almanack: The Wit and Wisdom of Charles T Munger*. Foreword by Warren Buffett. Donning, 2005.

## Other Must-Reads

Marcus Aurelius, *Meditations*. Penguin Classics, 2006.

Robert Cialdini, *Influence: The Psychology of Persuasion*. HarperBusiness, 2007.

Katharine Graham, *Personal History*. Weidenfeld & Nicolson, 2002.

Daniel Kahneman, *Thinking, Fast and Slow*. Penguin, 2012.

Robert Kiyosaki, *Second Chance: For Your Money, Your Life and Our World*. Plata Publishing, 2015.

Nassim Nicholas Taleb, *Fooled by Randomness*. Penguin, 2007.

William N Thorndike, Jr, *Outsiders: Eight Unconventional CEOs and Their Radically Rational Blueprint for Success*. Harvard Business Review Press, 2012.

Ashlee Vance, *Elon Musk: How the Billionaire CEO of SpaceX and Tesla is shaping our Future*. Virgin Books, 2015.